TWELVE
UNLIKELY HEROES

TWELVE
UNLIKELY HEROES

HOW GOD COMMISSIONED
UNEXPECTED PEOPLE in the BIBLE and
WHAT HE WANTS to DO with YOU

JOHN MACARTHUR

NELSON
BOOKS
An Imprint of Thomas Nelson

Published in Nashville, Tennessee, by Nelson Books, an imprint of Thomas Nelson. Nelson Books and Thomas Nelson are registered trademarks of HarperCollins Christian Publishing, Inc.

Thomas Nelson, Inc., titles may be purchased in bulk for educational, business, fund-raising, or sales promotional use. For information, please e-mail SpecialMarkets@ThomasNelson.com.

Unleashing God's Truth, One Verse at a Time® is a trademark of Grace to You. All rights reserved.

Unless otherwise noted, Scripture quotations are taken from THE NEW KING JAMES VERSION. © 1982 by Thomas Nelson, Inc. Used by permission. All rights reserved.

Scripture quotations marked NASB are from NEW AMERICAN STANDARD BIBLE®, © The Lockman Foundation 1960, 1962, 1963, 1968, 1971, 1972, 1973, 1975, 1977, 1995. Used by permission.

ISBN 978-1-4002-7484-0 (IE)
ISBN 978-1-4002-0611-7 (TP)

The Library of Congress has cataloged the hardcover edition as follows:

MacArthur, John, 1939–
Twelve unlikely heroes : how God commissioned unexpected people in the Bible and what he wants to do with you / by John MacArthur.
    p. cm.
Includes bibliographical references.
ISBN 978-1-4002-0208-9
1. Heroes in the Bible. 2. Bible--Biography. I. Title.
BS579.H4M33 2012
220.9'2--dc23

2012015176

Printed in the United States of America

15 16 17 18 RRD 12 11 10 9 8 7

DEDICATION

To my grandsons:
John Matthew
Ty Weston
Andrew Fullerton
Calvin Thomas
Oliver LeGrand

May God find in you faith and faithfulness so that He may add your name to the list of His unlikely heroes.

CONTENTS

Contents

INTRODUCTION

T HE WORD *HERO* IS SLOWLY LOSING its significance because it has been so broadly redefined in popular culture. Artificial heroes and imaginary heroes often overshadow real heroes. Some illusory ideas of heroism have found a home in pop culture. For example, a six-year-old is a hero if he pushes the ball past the fallen goalie in a soccer match so that his flock of ball chasers wins the game. A ten-year-old is a hero worthy of a bumper sticker if she is dubbed student of the week in her class—even if only because she was the one who gave the teacher the least grief. We even have grown-up versions of those same heroes in sports and entertainment.

Nowadays, celebrity status alone is enough to get a person deemed heroic. You'll often hear people refer to their favorite person as "my hero," indicating that all that may be necessary to be a hero is to have one person who thinks you are. There is even a mega-hit pop song in honor of someone's personal hero: "Wind Beneath My Wings." The song asks, "Did you ever know that you're my hero?" *Why?* Because "You were content to let me shine, that's your way. You always walked a step behind. So I was the one with all the glory"!

What? You are my hero because you gave me all the glory?

As bad as pop culture's relentless sentimentalizing and overuse (and thus cheapening) of the word *hero* is, our ideas of heroism are even more tarnished by our culture's ridiculous obsession with imaginary superheroes, whose fantasy exploits fill everything from comics and cartoons to television and movies. If the artificial heroes we invent in the name of self-esteem or celebrity lower the bar too far, then the imaginary heroes that exist only in fantasy worlds raise it too high. One approach trivializes heroism; the other mythologizes it.

Of course, there are *true* heroes in real life and always have been, but they do not gain that honor by scoring points in an artificial game meant to elevate their own egos. Nor do they earn it by manifesting the powers of an imaginary superhero. Real heroes are people whose efforts and sacrifices save lives, alter destinies, change history, or shift the course of history for the better.

They appear in vital roles of leadership—in war, medicine, science, law enforcement, civil service, education, or countless other everyday roles. They advance others' well-being in some significant way. Even people who don't know them and have no direct personal connection to them recognize their contributions. The world changes for the better because of them.

But even though they are true heroes, most of them make life better only in *this* world. Not beyond. The greatest heroes are those who are the human means God uses to change people forever—for their good and His glory. And these true heroes who make an eternal impact are invariably the most unexpected and ordinary people— God makes *unlikely* heroes.

Listen to what Paul wrote in 1 Corinthians 1:26–27:

> For you see your calling, brethren, that not many wise according to the flesh, not many mighty, not many noble, are called. But God has chosen the foolish things of the world to put to shame the

wise, and God has chosen the weak things of the world to put to shame the things which are mighty.

In other words, God works through people whom the world regards as weak, foolish, and unqualified. They are not self-reliant or self-sufficient. Instead, they are those unlikely believers who, when given unique opportunities for eternal impact, depend wholly on Him. As a result, His power and wisdom are put on display, overwhelming the shallow pretenses of worldly heroism.

THE MARKS OF A TRUE HERO

The pages of Scripture are filled with stories of great heroes—men and women whom God used in unique and powerful ways to accomplish His purposes. Their exploits vary greatly, yet the common thread that runs through all of their testimonies is *faith*.

Even though the word *hero* does not occur in the New Testament, believers often refer to the biblical saints (such as those listed in Hebrews 11) as the "heroes of the faith." They are regarded as heroes for two primary reasons: *they believed in the Lord*, not just for salvation but for every aspect of life; and they *acted on that faith*, choosing to honor Him even when it was difficult to do so. When their circumstances seemed impossible, they depended on God's wisdom and strength rather than their own. And they kept their eyes on Him, choosing to trust in His promises rather than pursue the passing pleasures of sin.

Thus, they were known both for their *faith* and their *faithfulness*—and God was honored through them. From the world's perspective, most of them were not especially noble, strong, or wise. They had quirks, flaws, and shortcomings. But through the power of God, they were used in mighty ways to accomplish His purposes and bring Him glory.

We have much to learn from the legacy left to us by the heroes of the faith. They are the great "cloud of witnesses" (Hebrews 12:1) that has gone before us. As we study their lives, their testimonies encourage us to respond to trials with steadfast faith and to fight against temptation with uncompromising faithfulness. Their circumstances were often far different from our own, and yet the God-centered principles and priorities that governed their lives are applicable to us as well.

It's true, the Lord worked through many of the biblical heroes in ways that were unique and extraordinary. We will never experience anything quite like walking through the Red Sea, defeating the Midianites with an army of only three hundred men, or saving the Jewish people from total annihilation. Nonetheless, we can learn a great deal from these faith-filled men and women and their noteworthy examples of courageous obedience. When we do, we will quickly find that being a hero doesn't require donning a cape or fist-fighting crime. It doesn't depend on celebrity-status, a high IQ, athletic talent, or lots of money. Instead, it starts with a rock-solid confidence in God and a willingness to live according to His Word no matter the consequences.

THE HERO BEHIND THE HEROES

At the outset of a book highlighting heroes of the faith, it is imperative to emphasize one critical point: the true hero of Scripture, in every Bible story, is God Himself. A quick review of several classic Sunday school stories immediately illustrates this point. Noah did not preserve the ark in the midst of the flood; Abraham did not make himself the father of a great nation; Joshua did not cause the walls of Jericho to fall down; and David did not defeat Goliath on his own. In each of those well-known examples, and in every other case, the Hero behind the heroes is always the Lord.

In literature, the hero is the main protagonist, the principal character, and the central figure of the narrative. That is certainly true of God throughout the pages of Scripture. He is the One who always provides the victory. It is His power, His wisdom, and His goodness that are continually put on display—even when He utilizes human instruments to accomplish His purposes. Consequently, all the glory belongs to Him.

As those who comprise the great cloud of witnesses, the human heroes of Scripture point us to Someone beyond themselves. He is the One to whom they continually looked in faith, and on whom they constantly depended. Their legacy of faithfulness ultimately directs our attention heavenward, to the Source of their wisdom and strength—namely, the Lord Himself. My prayer for you, as you read this book, is that you will fix your eyes firmly on Him (cf. Hebrews 12:2)—recognizing, along with all the heroes of the faith, that those who put their trust in Him will never be disappointed (Romans 10:11).

1
ENOCH: THE MAN WHO WALKED WITH GOD

———

Enoch walked with God; and he was not, for God took him.

—GENESIS 5:24

S OME HEROES ARE MADE IN A MOMENT. Others are defined by a lifetime. Such was certainly true of the fourth-century Christian leader, Athanasius, whose heroism was demonstrated over many decades by his unwavering refusal to compromise even when it seemed that all the world stood united against him.

Athanasius ministered in Alexandria, Egypt, during a time of epic transition within the Roman Empire. Emperor Constantine had recently put an end to the imperial policy of persecution against Christians. The church's newfound acceptance and rest, however, was short-lived. Danger and controversy soon threatened because of the subversive errors of a false teacher named Arius. At stake was no less than the biblical understanding of the deity of Christ and, consequently, the doctrine of the Trinity.

The truth about Christ's deity had always been an essential doctrine for the church, from the time of the apostles. But the heretic Arius arrogantly challenged that reality—brashly asserting that the

Son of God was merely a created being who was inferior rather than equal to God the Father. To make a modern comparison, Arius was the original Jehovah's Witness. He denied the deity of Christ and consequently destroyed the true gospel, replacing it with a damning substitute. Though his views were overwhelmingly denounced at the Council of Nicaea in 325, they remained popular even after his death in 336.

As early as 321, Athanasius (then only twenty-three years old) began writing against the false teachings of Arius. Seven years later, in 328, he became the pastor of the church in Alexandria—one of the most influential cities in the Roman Empire. Appropriately known as "the saint of stubbornness," Athanasius tirelessly dedicated his life and ministry to defending the deity of Christ and defeating the Arian heresy. But that courageous stand proved costly. The Arians were not only popular, they also had powerful political allies. Even Satan was on their side. As a result, Athanasius's life was constantly in danger. He was banished from Alexandria five different times, spending a total of seventeen years in exile—all because he resolutely refused to compromise. The unswerving pastor died in 373, after diligently guarding sound doctrine for more than half a century. And the Lord rewarded his faithfulness, enabling Athanasius to keep his finger in the dike for all those years to hold back the floodwaters of heresy at a critical point in the history of the church.

In the centuries since, a famous saying has been attributed to Athanasius though it can't be proven that he ever said it himself. The phrase in Latin is *Athanasius contra mundum*. It means, "Athanasius against the world" and it accurately epitomizes his lifelong stand against the widespread errors of Arianism. Though, at times, it appeared as if false teaching had swayed the entire Roman Empire, Athanasius would not compromise. During those long years in exile, when he felt almost completely alone, he refused to give in. And that is what made him a hero.

Enoch is rightly regarded as a hero for the same reason: he stood strong over a long period of time. Like Athanasius, he boldly opposed the false teachers of his day, courageously confronting the popular opinions of the society in which he lived (cf. Jude 14–15). Even in the midst of a corrupt and perverse civilization (one so wicked the Lord determined to destroy it in the Flood), Enoch refused to compromise. At times, he undoubtedly felt alone—as if the entire world were against him. Yet he remained true to the Lord. The author of Hebrews summed up Enoch's legacy with these profound words, "he pleased God" (Hebrews 11:5). Amazingly, he did so, not just for several decades, but for three hundred years!

A MAN WHO NEVER DIED

Throughout past generations of human history, out of the billions who have lived on this earth, only two people have never died. Though these remarkable individuals were separated by many centuries, their lives share striking similarities. Both were prophets of God; both warned the wicked of coming judgment; both lived at a time when following the Lord was utterly unpopular; and both went to heaven without experiencing physical death.

The second of these men, the prophet Elijah, boldly confronted the idol worship of his day, calling and challenging Israel to return to the true God. At times, he too felt alone—as if the whole world was against him (1 Kings 19:10). Yet he remained faithful. Though he lived in constant danger (and would have been killed if he were captured), Elijah survived until God sent a fiery chariot to transport him to his eternal home. One day while the seasoned prophet was walking with his student Elisha, "suddenly a chariot of fire appeared with horses of fire, and separated the two of them; and Elijah went up by a whirlwind into heaven" (2 Kings 2:11). As the startled Elisha stood watching dead in his tracks, his esteemed companion was whisked away by God. In a moment, with a rush of supernatural wind and a flash of blazing brilliance, he vanished, never to be seen on earth again—until he made a brief appearance in glorified form at the Transfiguration of Jesus (cf. Matthew 17:1–9).

Millennia earlier, another man was similarly taken by God from the earth. For three centuries, this godly preacher walked with the Lord in intimate fellowship and righteous obedience. His temporal journey ended one day while he was walking with God. Enoch, without dying, was suddenly snatched away to heaven.

The biblical account regarding Enoch consists of just a handful of verses found in Genesis, Hebrews, and Jude (along with mentions of his name in 1 Chronicles 1:3 and Luke 3:37). Even so, there is plenty of information given about him to include his amazing history in a book of heroes. In studying his life, we encounter an individual whose testimony was both extraordinary and exemplary. Though Enoch's experiences were remarkable and unique, he still sets a compelling example for us to follow: one of unwavering faith and uncompromising obedience.

A MAN WITH A NATURE LIKE OURS

Enoch's world was far different from ours. The earth had not yet been destroyed and rearranged into its present form by the Flood. Life expectancy was measured in centuries rather than in decades. Enoch himself was born only 622 years after creation, in the seventh generation from Adam. His son, Methuselah, lived longer than anyone else (at 969 years), and his great-grandson Noah, who famously built the ark, completed it at age 600.

The extended lifespans of this time were made possible by the ideal conditions on this pre-Flood planet. According to Genesis 1:6, a canopy of water completely encircled the atmosphere, thereby protecting earth's surface from the destructive effects of the sun's ultraviolet radiation. It also created a greenhouse-type environment that moderated climate and temperature, minimized winds and storms, and created the most favorable conditions for plant life. Additionally, in this lush tropical setting, rain was not necessary because the entire world was irrigated by a natural sprinkler system—a mist that came up from under the ground (Genesis 2:5–6).

Yet, in spite of its natural beauty and resources, the presence of sin in the pre-Flood world corrupted all who lived there. The effects of the Fall were felt immediately after Adam and Eve rebelled against God. Adam's oldest son, Cain, slaughtered his younger brother Abel in cold blood (Genesis 4:8). And the story gets worse. One of Cain's descendants—a man named Lamech—was, like Enoch, born in the seventh generation from Adam. Unlike Enoch, however, Lamech openly boasted of both murder and polygamy (Genesis 4:23). His flagrant lawlessness was characteristic of the civilization in which he lived. Three generations later, when the Lord "saw that the wickedness of man was great in the earth, and that every intent of the thoughts of his heart was only evil continually" (Genesis 6:5), He determined to drown the whole world.

In terms of topography, Enoch's world looked very different than ours does today. But the culture in which he lived was much the same—being characterized by comprehensive corruption, moral decay in every way possible, and open rebellion against God. The fact that people lived for so long was both a blessing and a curse. Their longer lifespans enabled them to develop intellectually and culturally at a rapid rate—which at the outset of human civilization was an important key to inhabiting and cultivating the riches of the earth (Genesis 1:28). At the same time, however, such longevity also accelerated the degradation of society. In our own day, we know how difficult it can be to battle temptation for seventy or eighty years. But those who sought to live godly lives in the pre-Flood era had to struggle against sin and endure its impact over many hundreds of years. That is what makes the examples of righteous men like Enoch so compelling: he stood against the corruption of his culture and walked with God for three centuries!

The legacy of Enoch's faithfulness is not only a monumental example for all believers to follow, but also a penetrating and enduring influence on his own family. That impact is especially evident in the life of his great-grandson Noah. Though Noah was born sixty-nine years after Enoch went to heaven, Enoch's testimony would have been passed down to him through his father and grandfather. According to Genesis 6:9, "Noah was a just man, perfect in his generations. Noah walked with God," just as his great-grandfather Enoch had done. Second Peter 2:5 describes Noah as a "preacher of righteousness," a role he undoubtedly learned from the accounts he heard of his great-grandfather's ministry (cf. Jude 14–15). Like Enoch, Noah confronted the corruption of his culture, and, like Enoch, Noah was miraculously saved by God from his evil society.

Enoch's remarkable life may seem, like Elijah's, an impossible one for us to emulate. Not so. Writing about Elijah, the apostle James told his readers, "Elijah was a man with a nature like ours" (James 5:17a). The same could also be said about Enoch. As a member of the sinful human race, Enoch fought against the same temptations, fears, and weaknesses that have plagued all men and women since the Fall. Even so, he was able to demonstrate enduring righteousness—not because he was sinless but because he drew on divine resources. He was a sinner who was saved by grace and empowered by the Holy Spirit to live by obedient faith. Thus, Enoch's righteous walk should not intimidate us. Rather, as a witness to the life of faith (Hebrews 12:1), his example ought to motivate us to greater faithfulness and deeper resolve in our own walk with the Lord.

A MAN WHO WALKED WITH GOD

Let's back up to the beginning of Enoch's story. He is first mentioned in the genealogical record of Genesis 5—a chapter that traces the righteous descendants of Adam from Seth all the way to Noah. As we might expect from a genealogy, Enoch is introduced in a way that is purely matter-of-fact: "Jared lived one hundred and sixty-two years, and begot Enoch" (Genesis 5:18). But Enoch's brief biography just a few verses later quickly makes it clear that his life was anything but ordinary. According to Genesis 5:21–24,

> Enoch lived sixty-five years, and begot Methuselah. After he begot Methuselah, Enoch walked with God three hundred years, and had sons and daughters. So all the days of Enoch were three hundred and sixty-five years. And Enoch walked with God; and he was not, for God took him.

In fewer than fifty words, the entire Old Testament account of Enoch's life is complete. Even so, there is much more here than mere genealogical data.

The genealogy of Genesis 5 is very important for at least two reasons. First, it indicates that Genesis 1–9 is real history, and it gives an accurate chronology of that time period. It is the true record of mankind from Adam to Noah (from God's creation of the world out of water to His destruction of it by water). Second, the genealogy chronicles death, as each obituary ends with the words, "and he died." The curse is in full force (Genesis 2:17), and for all those listed in the family tree, the end is always the same—with one notable exception. Enoch is set apart because he "walked with God" and because "he was not, for God took him." Let's examine both of those terse, but loaded, features of his life.

Twice in just four verses we are told that *Enoch walked with God*. In fact, that succinct phrase is all Genesis 5 tells us about the character of this man. But that's enough. Enoch lived in such a way that, after 365 years in this world, his life could be accurately summarized with repeated, sublime brevity. Nearly seven centuries after the Garden of Eden, when Adam and Eve had walked with God in perfection (cf. Genesis 3:8), there is finally someone who is said to commune with God in intimate, daily fellowship. And he did that for three hundred years.

To *walk with God* is another way to say that Enoch *pleased God*. In fact, the Septuagint—the Greek translation of the Hebrew Old Testament—renders the phrase exactly that way: "Enoch pleased God." The writer of Hebrews seals this meaning when he describes Enoch's life: "He had this testimony, that he pleased God" (Hebrews 11:5b). Because Enoch sought to be pleasing to God, God was well pleased to be in fellowship with him.

What can we learn practically about walking with God so that we can follow Enoch's example? Scripture, where this theme is reiterated and expanded, reveals that walking with God includes at least three component parts. It begins with forgiveness from sin, consists of faith in the Lord, and results in fruits of righteousness. Understanding these three aspects opens the door to the rich spiritual treasure that lies behind the simple words of Genesis 5.

THE STARTING POINT: FORGIVENESS FROM SIN

The Bible makes it clear that in order for sinful people to commune with a holy God, they must first be reconciled to Him from their alienated sinful condition.

In Amos 3:3, the prophet asked rhetorically, "Can two walk together, unless they are agreed?" The apostle Paul made a similar point in 2 Corinthians 6:14, "For what fellowship has righteousness with lawlessness? And what communion has light with darkness?" For sinners to be in agreement and harmony with the Lord whom they have rebelled against—and thereby to enjoy fellowship with Him—their sins must be forgiven and their hearts cleansed and made new. It may seem obvious, but it is important to state that Enoch was a saved man. He had, by divine grace, been forgiven for all his sin and transformed from God's enemy into His friend.

On what basis can a holy God forgive? How is that consistent with His perfect justice? For the answer, we go to Hebrews 11 where Enoch's example of saving faith is highlighted immediately after Abel's. The author of Hebrews says this about Adam's second-born son, "By faith Abel offered to God a more excellent sacrifice than Cain, through which he obtained witness that he was righteous" (Hebrews 11:4a). As Abel's example demonstrates, sinners must come to God in the way that He requires. In Abel's case, God required an animal sacrifice (Genesis 4:4), which Abel offered in faith. Such sacrifices were necessary as a vivid reminder that sin brings death and that fellowship with God requires an atonement (or covering) for sin. Though the sinner ought to die, an animal was killed as a substitute in his or her place.

Abel's sacrifice, as all Old Testament sacrifices, pointed to the cross, where Jesus Christ died once for all to make the only full and satisfactory atonement for sin. Because of Christ's death in their place, sinners can be forgiven and declared righteous by God apart from any moral goodness in them. With their sins paid for by Jesus' sacrifice, they are covered with His own righteousness. That imputed righteousness establishes reconciliation, enabling fallen human beings to enjoy fellowship with a holy God.

Like Abel, Enoch was a man who understood his own unworthiness and the need for a proper sacrifice. As truth was passed down from generation to generation among the godly descendants of Seth, Enoch would have learned about Abel's sacrificial offering. Clearly, he embraced the truth behind it, understanding that he was an undeserving sinner who needed a God-ordained substitute to bear the punishment in his place. His personal relationship with the Lord began when his sins were forgiven and he was covered by the righteousness of the Savior who would carry Enoch's sins to the cross and pay the penalty for them in full. Like all believers throughout every epoch of history, Enoch's testimony was one of salvation by grace through faith.

As a saved man, Enoch's life was characterized not by harsh legalism but by the joy of intimate communion with his Creator. People wrongly assume that the Old Testament focuses solely on rules, rituals, and ceremonies. But as Enoch's example demonstrates, the heart of true religion has always centered on constant fellowship with God. The Lord was Enoch's companion and confidant; and Enoch enjoyed daily, personal communion with Him.

Accordingly, the term *walk* expresses the idea of moment-by-moment fellowship with the Lord. And in the early chapters of Scripture, it is the primary way that someone is identified as having been forgiven from sin and reconciled to God. Because Noah walked with God, he escaped judgment (Genesis 6:9). Because Abraham walked with God, he received blessing (Genesis 17:1). Because Enoch walked with God, he avoided death.

That kind of fellowship is what God both desires and provides. It is that same kind of relationship that He still offers sinners today. As Jesus told the multitudes to whom He preached, "Come to Me, all you who labor and are heavy laden, and I will give you rest. Take My yoke upon you and learn from Me, for I am gentle and lowly in heart, and you will find rest for your souls" (Matthew 11:28–29). Even now, the Lord is looking for those who will come to Him for forgiveness—based on His substitutionary sacrifice—and walk with Him in fellowship.

THE SUBSTANCE: FAITH IN THE LORD

The author of Hebrews, in his account of Enoch's life, provides additional insight into what it means to walk with God.

> By faith Enoch was taken away so that he did not see death, "and was not found, because God had taken him"; for before he was taken he had this testimony, that he pleased God. But without faith it is impossible to please Him, for he who comes to God must believe that He is, and that He is a rewarder of those who diligently seek Him. (Hebrews 11:5–6)

Here the emphasis is on the spiritual substance of Enoch's walk—namely, faith in God. Apart from such faith, the sinner cannot be reconciled to God or have fellowship with Him. As Ephesians 2:8–9 states so clearly, "For by grace you have been saved through faith, and that not of yourselves; it is the gift of God, not of works, lest anyone should boast."

Hebrews 11:6 denotes two defining characteristics of those who, like Enoch, possess true saving faith. First, "he who comes to God must believe that He is." In other words, the sinner must affirm the true God as He really is. Belief in a god of one's own imagination, or in the generic concept of a higher power, is not sufficient. Saving faith finds its object in the true God alone as revealed in Scripture.

How can we know the truth about God and salvation? It is only because He has made it known in His Word. Even in Enoch's day, in the first millennium of human history, the Lord had disclosed saving truth about Himself and His righteous requirements to the people of that time (cf. Jude 14–15). Enoch embraced that truth and placed his faith firmly in the true God. If we are to walk with the Lord, we, too, must wholeheartedly embrace Him as He has revealed Himself in His Word.

Second, those who would walk in faith must believe that God "is the rewarder of those who diligently seek Him." That is to say, they must trust in Him as their Redeemer and Savior—believing that He will fulfill His promises to those who put their hope in Him. One day, their faith will be rewarded with sight and their hope will be realized in eternal glory. That kind of confidence characterized the faith of Enoch, and it is the mark of those who walk with God.

The fact that God is a Savior and Redeemer sets Christianity apart from every other religion in the world. Whereas false gods are indifferent, distant, cruel, and harsh, the true and living God is a reconciler and rewarder by nature, as 1 John 4:8–10 explains,

He who does not love does not know God, for God is love. In this the love of God was manifested toward us, that God has sent

His only begotten Son into the world, that we might live through Him. In this is love, not that we loved God, but that He loved us and sent His Son to be the propitiation for our sins.

Because of His infinite love, God is a lavish rewarder of those who put their faith in Him. As Paul told the Ephesians, "Blessed be the God and Father of our Lord Jesus Christ, who has blessed us with every spiritual blessing in the heavenly places in Christ" (Ephesians 1:3). He grants sinners forgiveness, clothes them in His righteousness, and creates in them a new heart. God turns former rebels into His children, giving them His Spirit, His blessings, and the promise of eternal life. He has provided the only way for unworthy sinners to have fellowship with Him through His Son Jesus Christ (John 14:6); and all who come, He will not turn away. As Christ Himself said, "All that the Father gives Me will come to Me, and the one who comes to Me I will by no means cast out" (John 6:37).

Enoch's walk with the Lord was marked by steadfast faith in the true God. He put his confidence in God's gracious forgiveness and imputed righteousness, knowing that his hope in the Lord would not be disappointed. According to Hebrews 11:5, Enoch's life was characterized "by faith" even to the end. Faith is the substance of the redeemed life. It was for Enoch, and it must be for us as well.

THE SUBSEQUENT RESULT: FRUITS OF RIGHTEOUSNESS

Walking with God is characterized by forgiveness from sin and faith in the Lord. Third, it produces the spiritual fruit of a transformed life. One of the primary evidences of genuine salvation is a sincere desire, on the part of the converted, to know God intimately and obey Him fully. The last line in Hebrews 11:6 notes that those who please God "diligently seek Him." That seeking does not end at the moment of conversion, but represents a lifelong desire to grow deeper in relationship with Him. Enoch walked with God for three hundred years. The implication is that, over all those years, he was growing in communion with God, continually seeking to know Him more perfectly.

The concept of seeking implies being purposeful and focused; it is an intentional and passionate pursuit. That kind of diligence characterized all those whom Scripture describes as having walked with God—including Enoch, Noah, Abraham, Moses, Joshua, David, Hezekiah, and Josiah. They earnestly desired to know God, and as a result, they pursued Him with every fiber of their being.

They also understood that to walk with God includes living in loving obedience to Him. As the Lord told the Israelites, while they were camped at Mount Sinai, "If you walk in My statutes and keep My commandments, and perform them . . . I will walk among you and be your God, and you shall be My people" (Leviticus 26:3, 12). To walk in fellowship with God is to "love the LORD your God with all your heart, with all your soul, with all your mind, and with all your strength" (Mark 12:30). That kind of all-consuming love assumes obedience. As the Lord Jesus told His disciples in the Upper Room, "If you love Me, keep My commandments" (John 14:15). A few verses later, He reiterated that point with these words, "You are My friends if you do whatever I command you" (John 15:14).

The concept of walking with God, a prominent theme in the Old Testament, is continued in the New. Believers are commanded to walk in a manner worthy of the Lord. They are not to walk according to the flesh or their former way of life, but rather, according to the Spirit, in newness of life, in love, in good works, and in truth. They are to walk by faith, as children of light, and in keeping with God's commandments. Jesus Himself was the ultimate example of one who lived every moment in perfect communion and intimate fellowship with His Father. He sets the pattern for us to follow. As 1 John 2:6 reminds us, "He who says he abides in Him ought himself also to walk just as He walked."

Like believers in Bible times, all Christians are called to walk in obedience, truth, and godliness. Of course, everything in society fights that effort. Secular culture is only getting worse, and the church, in many cases, has grown weak and shallow. The temptation to compromise and sin is immense and relentless. But as in the days of Enoch and Noah, God is watching for those who will faithfully walk with Him. As 2 Chronicles 16:9 reminds us, "The eyes of the LORD run to and fro throughout the whole earth, to show Himself strong on behalf of those whose heart is loyal to Him." The actions of godly men and women are not determined by peer pressure or popular opinion. Rather, they arise from deep personal character and conviction—the kind forged over years of walking with the Lord in fellowship, truth, and obedience.

That kind of walk characterized Enoch's life. It started with forgiveness from sin. It was marked by steadfast faith in the Lord. And it subsequently resulted in fruits of righteousness. In the midst of a corrupt society headed for total destruction, Enoch's walk with God was counter-cultural and heavenly in character, as his earthly end demonstrates.

A MAN WHO PREACHED THE TRUTH

Like any godly person would be, Enoch was deeply disturbed over the spiritual ruin of the souls in his society. And he took action to warn them about God's impending judgment.

Genesis 5:21 indicates that Enoch named his son "Methuselah"—a name that means either "man of the javelin" or "man of the sending forth." Evidently, the Lord had revealed to Enoch that judgment would be suddenly unleashed on the earth (sent forth like a javelin), but that it would not come until after Methuselah died. Thus, even the name of Enoch's son was a warning to the world of his day. The fact that God allowed Methuselah to live almost a thousand years—

longer than any other person in history—showcases the fact that He is indeed gracious and patient toward sinners (cf. 2 Peter 3:9).

Enoch was sixty-five years old when Methuselah was born. According to Genesis 5:22, it was at that point in his life when Enoch really began to walk with God. Perhaps this was due to the realization that divine judgment was imminent. But whatever the cause, from that event on, he diligently sought the Lord, and he also sought salvation for the people around him, warning them of the wrath of God that would fall on the ungodly.

The apostle Jude gives us a glimpse into the content of Enoch's preaching. In Jude 14–15, we read:

> Now Enoch, the seventh from Adam, prophesied about these men also, saying, "Behold, the LORD comes with ten thousands of His saints, to execute judgment on all, to convict all who are ungodly among them of all their ungodly deeds which they have committed in an ungodly way, and of all the harsh things which ungodly sinners have spoken against Him."

Jude wrote as a warning against false teachers who were attempting to creep into the church, but he makes it clear that this was not a new threat. Since Satan's fall, there have always been false teachers, and they were present in Enoch's lifetime—those who had gone "the way of Cain" (Jude v. 11) by advocating wickedness, immorality, and rebellion against God. The prophetic warning given by Enoch fit Jude's message so well that the Holy Spirit inspired Jude to use it as a parallel.

Enoch's trumpet blast of impending doom was a bold contrast to the false comfort that blanketed the ungodly culture of his day. Although this prophecy was not recorded in the book of Genesis, the Holy Spirit revealed it to the apostle Jude so he could include it in his letter. As such, we can rest confidently in its historical veracity. Enoch's message in Jude vv. 14–15 is actually the oldest human spoken prophecy recorded in Scripture. His words, though found at the end of the Bible, predate the preaching of Noah, Moses, Samuel, and the other Old Testament prophets by many centuries.

Jude took this quote from an extra-biblical book called *1 Enoch* that was included in the written tradition of the Jewish people. By citing that book, Jude was not implying that he endorsed everything in it. But he did affirm that this particular quotation was indeed part of Enoch's original message. In the same way that the apostle Paul cited pagan Greek poets to make a point in Acts 17:28, Jude quoted here from a well-known Jewish source in order to emphasize the certainty of God's judgment against the ungodly.

Enoch's sober warning emphasized four realities regarding God's judgment on the wicked. First, he focused on God as the Judge, noting that the Lord Himself would come to punish the ungodly. When destruction began to be unleashed, there would be no question as to who was behind it. In the Greek original, the verb *comes* is actually in the past tense, indicating that Enoch was so certain of the Lord's involvement that he spoke of it as though it had already happened.

Second, Enoch explained that the Lord would not come by Himself. Though He alone is the ultimate Judge, He would be accompanied by heavenly multitudes sent to execute His judgments. The word translated *saints* actually means "holy ones" in Greek. In the context, it is better understood as holy angels, since in Scripture angels often accompany the Lord in judgment. Enoch's prophecy indicates that angels played a part in the devastation that was unleashed at the Flood. They will also be involved in the deadly destruction of the world at the end of human history.

Third, Enoch's warning underscored the fact that God's wrath had a definite purpose, which was to execute judgment upon all the ungodly. Those who had disregarded God's law, actively demonstrating the depraved nature of their hearts, would be justly punished by their offended and dishonored Creator. The verb rendered *to convict* means "to expose" or "to prove guilty." The Lord's judgment on wicked men was not random, uncontrolled, or unprovoked. It was a targeted response to the open rebellion and rank iniquity of every single violation in the sinful world.

Fourth, Enoch made it clear that God's judgment was well deserved by those on whom it fell. Enoch used the word *ungodly* four different times to describe the wicked on whom the Lord brought judgment. They were ungodly in their attitudes, actions, motives, and words. As a holy and righteous Judge, God was right to punish them. They had stored up divine wrath for themselves (Romans 2:5)—everything they did, including every intention of their hearts, was continually evil (Genesis 6:5).

For three hundred years, this was the theme of Enoch's prophetic message. Without question, his personal walk with God would have been evident in the power of his fervent preaching. He faithfully warned the world about the coming wrath of God. Even though he would never see that judgment himself, Enoch boldly proclaimed it nonetheless. Those who walk most closely with God most passionately warn sinners of His coming judgment. Three generations later, Enoch's great-grandson Noah took up that same mantle (2 Peter 2:5). When the first raindrops began to fall and the Flood waters started to rise, no one could claim that they had not been repeatedly forewarned.

Though Enoch's prophecy was initially fulfilled in that great deluge, it ultimately looked beyond the Flood—to Christ's future return and God's coming judgment of this fallen planet. In the past, God drowned the world with water, but ultimately this earth will be destroyed by fire (2 Peter 3:10–12). As such, Enoch's words still serve as a sobering warning in our own day. The Lord Jesus Christ will certainly return with the hosts of heaven, and when He does, He will punish the ungodly who neither believe in Him nor obey His gospel (2 Thessalonians 1:7–10).

A MAN WHO WALKED INTO HEAVEN

During his life, Enoch was characterized by intimate fellowship with God, personal integrity, and faithful preaching. But it is his dramatic, death-free exit that sets Enoch apart. The Genesis account draws the final curtain with cryptic terseness, stating simply that "he was not, for God took him" (Genesis 5:24b). Importantly, the Hebrew expression "took him" does not mean to "take someone's life" in the sense of killing a person or causing an untimely death. Rather, it has the same sense as the word *rapture*, meaning to "snatch away" or "take up" to heaven. In the New Testament, Hebrews 11:5 expands our understanding of what happened to this godly man: "By faith Enoch was taken away so that he did not see death, 'and was not found, because God had taken him.'"

That is an incredible statement! One day during his 365th year, Enoch suddenly disappeared. He vanished from this earth without a trace. He took a walk with God and never came back. He just walked from earth past the entire universe and stepped into heaven. For the first time in human history, there was no obituary because there was no death to record. According to some Jewish traditions, Enoch was escorted to heaven in the same way as Elijah. But that is only speculation since the Bible does not give us any details.

Significantly, Enoch's incredible transport to heaven prefigured the rapture event that believers will experience when Christ comes for His bride, the church. At that time, all the saved will be miraculously transported to meet their Savior in the air and then be escorted by Him to heaven. As Paul told the Thessalonians,

> For the Lord Himself will descend from heaven with a shout, with the voice of an archangel, and with the trumpet of God. And the dead in Christ will rise first. Then we who are alive and remain shall be caught up together with them in the clouds to meet the Lord in the air. And thus we shall always be with the Lord. (1 Thessalonians 4:16–17)

Amazingly, at the rapture of the church, there will be a whole generation of Enochs—those who will not taste death because they are snatched away by God. In that moment, in "the twinkling of an eye," they will hear the voice of the archangel and the trumpet of God, and they will receive their resurrection bodies (1 Corinthians 15:52). Like Enoch, they will not die, but will disappear from the earth before God's judgment is unleashed.

The "twinkling of an eye" is not a blink, but the time it takes for a flash of light to reflect on the eye! That is the speed with which believers will go from earth to meet their Savior, and it was surely the speed with which Enoch went from this planet to paradise. In atomic science, a "quantum leap" describes the nearly instantaneous jumping of an electron from one energy level to another, seemingly without traversing the space in between. When Christ comes for His church, believers will take a quantum leap into heaven.

As with all the heroes of the faith listed in Hebrews 11, Enoch's life is notable not because of what he did, but because of how God's glory and greatness were displayed through him. Much about Enoch's life was unexpected and extraordinary. Yet he still has much to teach us, which is why the Bible includes him as an example of saving faith and personal integrity. In the midst of a wicked generation, Enoch fellowshipped with God constantly. For three centuries, he resisted the world's corruption, sought the Lord diligently, and lived in obedience to Him. Moreover, he understood that "friendship with the world is enmity with God" (James 4:4). As the friend of God, Enoch confronted the corruption that characterized his culture and warned sinners of the judgment that awaits all who persist in ungodliness. In the end, God honored Enoch to show His pleasure with such faithful virtue.

Though we may not escape death in this life (unless we are alive when the Lord calls the church at the Rapture), we possess the same hope that Enoch had. As those who have put our faith in Jesus Christ, walking with Him in full forgiveness and intimate fellowship, we can rest assured that we have received eternal life. We are no longer under the wrath of God, nor will we ever face His condemnation

(Romans 8:1). Though we may die, the sting of death has been removed, replaced by the hope of resurrection life. For us, to be absent from the body is to be instantly and eternally present with the Lord (cf. 2 Corinthians 5:8; Philippians 1:21).

Enoch's walk with God did not end when he stepped into heaven. It became perfect! So will ours. For eternity, we will enjoy glorious fellowship with our Lord and Savior as we worship and serve Him in the infinite wonder of His matchless presence.

2

JOSEPH: BECAUSE GOD MEANT IT FOR GOOD

But as for you, you meant evil against me; but God meant it for good, in order to bring it about as it is this day, to save many people alive.

—GENESIS 50:20

ELEVEN GRIM FACES STARED ANXIOUSLY DOWN at the floor. Though all eyes were on the ground, all attention was focused on the man enthroned at the front of the room. Huddled in tense silence, the eleven knelt before one of the most powerful rulers in the land, knowing he had the authority to execute them.

Garbed in distinctive fashion fitting his office and flanked by guards and servants, the prime minister looked down on these humble herdsmen as they stooped before him. His long history with these men included especially vivid memories of pain and rejection. They had wronged him unthinkably in the past. Now the tables were turned. With a word, he could enact severe retribution on those who had betrayed him.

Is that the action Joseph would take against his brothers? Their father Jacob had just died, and together they had buried him. Now they were bowing before their brother and begging him for mercy, fearful that, with their father's passing, Joseph might finally seek revenge against them for the severe cruelty they had perpetrated against him decades earlier.

Minutes felt like hours in the somber anticipation of Joseph's decision. The brothers braced themselves for the worst. Reuben, the oldest, had long blamed himself for what had happened to Joseph. Judah, too, felt the stinging weight of guilt; he was the one who had initially suggested selling Joseph into slavery. But all the brothers—except for Benjamin, the youngest—had been involved in that unthinkable act of treachery. They were all blameworthy. Was this the day their crimes had finally caught up with them?

When the silence was broken, it was not with a voice of angry threats or harsh punishment. Instead, it was the sound of weeping. The brothers' gloomy expressions softened with bewilderment. One by one, they slowly lifted their gazes, curious to see what was happening. Joseph looked back at them with a forgiving smile, tears tumbling down his face. His tears proved contagious, as they all wept.

Struggling to regain his composure, Joseph collected himself long enough to release the compassion that was in his heart. The Genesis account records his words:

"Do not be afraid, for am I in the place of God? But as for you, you meant evil against me; but God meant it for good, in order to bring it about as it is this day, to save many people alive. Now therefore, do not be afraid; I will provide for you and your little ones." And he comforted them and spoke kindly to them. (Genesis 50:19–21)

Unlike those who breed a seething hatred and desire for vengeance, Joseph treated his brothers with undeserved favor. But how do kindness and love get cultivated in the heart of one so wickedly treated? The answer is found in Joseph's theology—he had a clear understanding of God's providence. In that moment, with his brothers before him and his trials behind him, Joseph articulated a perspective that summarized the story of his life: *God is in control and we can trust Him for the outcome.*

Joseph's story has been retold many times and in many ways— from dramatic productions of technicolor dreamcoats to cartoon specials featuring talking vegetables. Spiritual lessons about brotherly love, moral purity, good stewardship, and patient perseverance have all been drawn from Joseph's life. Those are helpful lessons to learn, but they are not the reason that Joseph's experiences are recorded for us in the Bible. Until we see the big picture of what God was doing through Joseph, we will inevitably miss the profound and foundational truth the account of this unlikely hero teaches us.

Joseph didn't miss that truth. And he summarized it in the verses cited above. Bottom line—the Lord used Joseph's suffering to accomplish His sovereign purposes. To be sure, God had some practical life-lessons for Joseph to learn along the way. But He had a far bigger matter on His mind: a plan for His chosen people—one that included sparing them from a severe seven-year famine, then bringing them to Egypt where, over the next four centuries, they would be transformed from a family into a nation to witness His glory. It was all part of God's plan to fulfill His covenant promises of a seed and salvation that would extend to the whole earth (cf. Genesis 12:1–3).

As New Testament believers looking back on Joseph's example, we can see the principle of Romans 8:28 fleshed out in his life: "And we know that all things work together for good to those who love God, to those who are the called according to His purpose." As Joseph himself articulated, God intended the trials of his life for the good of his people, and though Joseph did not suffer because God was punishing him for sin, he *did* suffer so that God could ultimately save sinners.

A FAMILY FEUD

Joseph's painful journey in the good purpose of God began when he was only seventeen years old and still living in the land of Canaan with his father and his older half-brothers. Though they were all sons of Jacob (whose name God had changed to *Israel* in Genesis 32:28), Joseph's ten older brothers were not born through his mother Rachel. Only he and his younger brother Benjamin shared the same mother, and she had died when Benjamin was born.

The environment in which Joseph grew up was filled with family tension and strife. Conflict ran in the family. His father Jacob had tricked his own father Isaac in order to cheat his brother Esau out of the family birthright. Joseph's maternal grandfather, Laban, was also upset at Jacob for trying to sneak away from the homestead in Haran. His mother, Rachel, was in a constant jealousy war with her older sister, Leah. In a race to have more children, Leah and Rachel gave Jacob their handmaidens as concubines, which further complicated family relationships. When the family moved to Canaan, two of Joseph's half-brothers, Simeon and Levi, murdered an entire village to seek revenge for their sister, Dinah—causing deep distress for their father and strained relations with their new neighbors. Joseph's oldest brother, Reuben, even had an affair with one of his father's concubines, which Jacob later heard about. Needless to say, Joseph's home life was loaded with bad relations. Things did not get any easier for the young man when his mother passed away, or when his brothers began to treat him with hostility and resentment. Yet out of the turmoil, God would fulfill His plans for this feuding family, for Joseph in particular, for the nation of Israel, and for the world.

According to Genesis 37, Joseph's brothers hated him for several reasons. The core of the problem was that he was their father's favorite son (v. 3). Jacob had played favorites before with Rachel, Joseph's mother, and now, he treated her son with greater favor than the others. In the same way that Leah had been envious of her sister

Rachel, Joseph's brothers grew jealous of him. To show his singular affection for Joseph, Jacob gave him a royal robe. Whether or not it was actually a coat *of many colors* is debated by biblical commentators; the Hebrew word may actually refer to a coat with long sleeves or a long hem around the ankles. But whatever its appearance, it was given as a symbol of Joseph's favored status, and it ended up being a symbol of his brothers' contempt for him.

The whole scene escalated as Joseph appeared to his brothers to act like royalty. Not only was he wearing a kingly robe, they thought he was starting to talk and act like a superior. His father had also elevated him to the responsibility of keeping tabs on his brothers' work, and Joseph had no hesitation about returning with a bad report concerning them (Genesis 37:2). Even more offensive were his accounts of seemingly outrageous dreams, in which his brothers paid homage to him, and about which he seemed more than happy to tell them. One day, he met his brothers with the following dream announcement:

> "There we were, binding sheaves in the field. Then behold, my sheaf arose and also stood upright; and indeed your sheaves stood all around and bowed down to my sheaf." And his brothers said to him, "Shall you indeed reign over us? Or shall you indeed have dominion over us?" So they hated him even more for his dreams and for his words. (Genesis 37:7–8)

A second dream—in which the sun, moon, and stars bowed down before him—only made his envious brothers more irate. Their young half-brother, whom they undoubtedly viewed as spoiled by an over-fed ego, had finally gone too far. The biblical account never attributes pride to Joseph even in sharing his dreams; perhaps he was relaying them because he believed God gave them for him to report to his fellow family members. Nonetheless, his brothers' hatred was fed by the dreams. They began seeking the opportunity to divest the dreamer of both his royal robe and his place in the family.

That opportunity knocked on a day when Joseph's brothers were feeding their flocks in Dothan, and he was sent to check on them. The journey was not a short one since Dothan was located sixty-three miles away. It would have taken Joseph several days to reach them.

His brothers saw him coming from a distance, and their fomenting hatred formed into a deadly plan.

Now when they saw him afar off, even before he came near them, they conspired against him to kill him. Then they said to one another, "Look, this dreamer is coming! Come therefore, let us now kill him and cast him into some pit; and we shall say, 'Some wild beast has devoured him.' We shall see what will become of his dreams!" (Genesis 37:18–20)

If it were not for Reuben's intervention—suggesting that it was better to throw him in a pit alive—Joseph's brothers would have murdered him on the spot. As the oldest brother, Reuben was responsible to protect his brother. Genesis 37:22 explains that he planned to come back to the pit and rescue Joseph.

When Jacob's favorite son arrived, his brothers grabbed him, stripped him of his special robe, and dumped him into a dry well. The large, bottle-shaped pit was cut deep into the rock. It had a small opening at the top, just large enough for a water bucket (or a teenage boy) to pass through. Farther down, the narrow passage opened into a sizeable chasm. The slippery walls, which were plastered to ensure that no water escaped, would have also made it impossible for Joseph to escape on his own. Scared and confused, he offered cries for help from inside his dark prison. But his brothers paid no attention to his pleas.

Instead, they decided to have lunch. As they sat down to eat and determine what to do with Joseph, they spotted a caravan of merchants passing by. That caravan presented a new option, so Judah said to his brothers, "What profit is there if we kill our brother and conceal his blood? Come and let us sell him" (Genesis 37:26–27a).

After some negotiations, they settled on a price of twenty pieces of silver (the average price for a male slave at this time). The terrified teenager was hoisted out of the pit and handed over to the group of North Arabian traders headed for Egypt. Joseph continued to plead with his brothers, but it was hopeless (cf. Genesis 42:21). They wanted him gone permanently.

Joseph had descended from being the favored son to being a kidnapped slave. Surely he wondered why God permitted this to happen. And how did this fit with the dreams God had given him? Without warning, he had become a victim of "human trafficking." At seventeen, Joseph's whole world was flipped on its head. Betrayed by his brothers, he had the joys of home and the security of his father's love violently ripped away from him. Since we know the end of the story, we also know that while the Lord never condones evil, He does overrule it and accomplish His purpose out of it.

Reuben, who had wandered off, didn't return to the pit until Joseph was gone. As the firstborn, Reuben knew that Jacob would hold him personally responsible for all that had happened. In distress and dismay, he tore his clothes, and, in stark fear of his father's anger, said to his brothers, "The lad is no more; and I, where shall I go?" (Genesis 37:30).

They all knew that they needed to avoid their father's wrath, so they concocted an elaborate lie. First, they killed a goat, then they dipped Joseph's robe in its blood. The idea was to deceive their father into thinking it was Joseph's blood and wild animals had killed him. Ironically, Jacob had fooled his father Isaac using a goat skin years earlier (Genesis 27:16).

When he saw Joseph's bloodstained robe, Jacob slumped into a prolonged depression, mourning the loss of his son. His other sons tried to console him, but he refused to be comforted. Guilt must have eaten away at Reuben, and probably at the other brothers as well (cf. Genesis 42:22), but it was mitigated by the fact that they were rid of their brother, finally and for good. Or so they thought.

A FALSE ACCUSATION

Meanwhile, Joseph was taken down to Egypt, where he was sold as a slave to Potiphar, a chief servant of Pharaoh. However, in the purposes of God and by means of Joseph's natural qualities of leadership, he quickly rose to a position of prominence in Potiphar's house. Joseph was so capable and trustworthy that his master gladly put all his possessions in Joseph's care. The same qualities that made him the favored son of his father made him the favored slave of his master.

It was God's providence that Joseph be placed in Potiphar's house. His master was part of Pharaoh's court, which allowed Joseph to be introduced to royalty and the noble customs of Egypt. Such knowledge would later prove essential. Joseph was also given a unique opportunity to develop his leadership qualities. Instead of merely reporting on his brothers' activities (as he had done back in Canaan), he was now directly managing his master's resources. That administrative experience would likewise prove invaluable for Joseph's future. Joseph's placement in Potiphar's house also ensured that, if he were ever found guilty of a crime, he would be sent to the same place where Pharaoh's own prisoners were confined (cf. Genesis 39:20). That, too, was crucial to the divine plan.

The plot thickened, however, when Potiphar's wife began to take an illicit interest in her husband's Hebrew slave. The biblical text notes that Joseph was handsome in appearance (Genesis 39:6), and Potiphar's responsibilities, as a member of Pharaoh's court, likely kept him away from home often and for extended periods. Some commentators have further suggested that he may even have been a eunuch. In any case, driven by her own lustful desires, Potiphar's wife repeatedly attempted to seduce Joseph, and he repeatedly rejected her every attempt.

Joseph acknowledged his master's absence when he responded to his would-be seductress. According to Genesis 39:8–9,

He refused and said to his master's wife, "Look, my master does not know what is with me in the house, and he has committed all that he has to my hand. There is no one greater in this house than I, nor has he kept back anything from me but you, because you are his wife. How then can I do this great wickedness, and sin against God?"

Joseph assessed the situation correctly. To consent to her wishes would not only would have betrayed his master's trust, but would have been an egregious offense against the Lord Himself.

One of those days when Joseph was alone in the house, the woman cornered him and grabbed hold of his tunic. In an immediate effort to escape, Joseph ran out of the garment, leaving it in her hands. For the second time in his life, he was stripped of his clothing. When his brothers grabbed his robe, he was thrown into a pit. This time, his garment in the hands of Potiphar's wife would result in his being thrown into prison.

Scorned by his refusal, her sensual desires for pleasure with Joseph immediately turned into vicious animosity. Her fury raged against Joseph, and she shouted to the other servants in the house. When they found her, she accused Joseph of attempted rape, holding up his garment as proof.

Joseph was innocent, of course. But he had no alibi, and she had his clothes. It was his word against hers, and when the master came home, it was Potiphar's slave and not Potiphar's wife who went to prison. Significantly, however, Joseph was not put to death for his alleged crimes. Normally in ancient Egypt, adultery was a capital offense. The fact that he was merely thrown in jail may indicate that, even though Potiphar was angry, he knew Joseph's character and was not fully convinced of the credibility of his wife. So Joseph was bound and taken captive again.

Once more, Joseph must have wondered how all these really bad things could be happening to him when he had done nothing to deserve such treatment. In fact, in the face of great temptation, he had continually responded by honoring the Lord and doing what was right. From the human perspective, his circumstances seemed completely unfair. He couldn't know at this time that God had Joseph exactly where He wanted him. The Lord was perfectly in control.

A FORGETFUL FRIEND

It sounds strange, but even in prison Joseph experienced the Lord's blessing. His administrative skills were noticed by the warden, and soon he was placed in charge of all prison operations. Joseph was so competent and efficient that, according to Genesis 39:23, "the keeper of the prison did not look into anything that was under Joseph's authority, because the LORD was with him; and whatever he did, the LORD made it prosper."

Archaeological evidence from this period indicates that, within the Egyptian penal system, one of the positions under the prison warden was called the "scribe of the prison," who was responsible to keep all the prison records. Given Joseph's experience working for Potiphar and the biblical description of his role while incarcerated, it is likely that Joseph attained such a position of prominence, giving him access to all incoming prisoners, including those from the royal court.

After some royal intrigue, Pharaoh's cupbearer (sometimes translated as *butler*) and chief baker arrived at the prison. The biblical account does not indicate the nature of their alleged crimes, except to say that they had greatly offended the king. It is likely that they were suspected of treason related to a plot to poison the king. Why else would the heads of Pharaoh's food preparation staff be thrown in prison? And why else would the chief baker be hanged to death? Whatever the nature of their crimes, the baker and the cupbearer were put in prison to await Pharaoh's verdict.

One night, each man had a dream so troubling and extraordinary that the next day they were still upset. When Joseph asked the cause of their consternation, each reiterated his dream. In response, Joseph revealed the correct interpretation of each dream—a life-changing message of restoration for the cupbearer and a life-ending message of condemnation for the baker.

The Genesis account makes it clear that God was the one who gave the men their dreams and Joseph the interpretation. Like Daniel centuries later, Joseph knew that he had no ability to tell the future (Daniel 2:27–30). The Lord revealed the true interpretation so that His power might be displayed and His purposes fulfilled.

After interpreting the cupbearer's dream, Joseph specifically asked the man not to forget about him. In Genesis 40:14–15, he said to the cupbearer, "Remember me when it is well with you, and please show kindness to me; make mention of me to Pharaoh, and get me out of this house. For indeed I was stolen away from the land of the Hebrews; and also I have done nothing here that they should put me into the dungeon." Twice before, Joseph had been unjustly treated by other people: first, by his own brothers and then by Potiphar's wife. This time he entrusted himself to Pharaoh's cupbearer. Again, he would be let down. The cupbearer was indeed restored to Pharaoh's service, but he was indifferent to Joseph's plight. The fortieth chapter of Genesis ends with this final sentence, "Yet the chief butler did not remember Joseph, but forgot him" (v. 23).

For two more years, Joseph suffered the deprivation and indignities of prison. Since the cupbearer had promised to put in a good word for him, Joseph was likely optimistic for the first weeks and months. Maybe he would receive word from the court of Pharaoh bringing a pardon. Nothing came. As the months rolled into years, the Hebrew prisoner came to grips with the fact that he had been mistreated by another man he had trusted.

But God had neither forgotten nor abandoned Joseph. Nor would the Lord allow the cupbearer's amnesia to last indefinitely. The time was coming when Pharaoh would need someone who could interpret dreams. Right on cue, in the unfolding of this divinely ordained drama, the cupbearer would remember his extraordinary prison experience. God's plan for Joseph was coming together exactly as He intended.

A FAMINE FORETOLD

One night Pharaoh awoke in a cold sweat, startled by the most vivid and terrible nightmare he had ever experienced. In his dream, Pharaoh found himself on the banks of the Nile River, with seven beautiful, healthy cows feeding in a meadow nearby. The scene was peaceful and serene. Suddenly, like something from a bovine horror movie, seven skinny cows rushed into the field, attacked the fat cows, and ate them! Even after devouring the fat cows, the skinny cows remained as ugly and gaunt as before. Pharaoh responded to the dream by waking with a start—undoubtedly sitting up in his bed and staring into the darkness. What did this mean? Finally, tossing and turning, he drifted back into a troubled sleep only to dream again. His second nightmare repeated the same shocking pattern as the first, except instead of cows, seven plump heads of grain were gobbled up by seven thin, withered heads.

The next day, Pharaoh was deeply troubled. He was even more distraught when none of his magicians or wise men could tell him what the dream meant. The alarming situation was enough to jog the cupbearer's poor memory so that he remembered Joseph, the one who had interpreted his dream. Pharaoh wasted no time in securing Joseph's release. He was given a change of clothes and a quick shave, and was rushed into Pharaoh's presence.

And Pharaoh said to Joseph, "I have had a dream, and there is no one who can interpret it. But I have heard it said of you that you can understand a dream, to interpret it." So Joseph answered

Pharaoh, saying, "It is not in me; God will give Pharaoh an answer of peace." (Genesis 41:15–16)

After the king recounted his dream, the Lord revealed the interpretation of it through Joseph. Both dreams depicted the same future reality—there would be seven years of plenty followed by seven years of famine. If the Egyptians were to be ready for the coming catastrophe, they would have to begin storing up resources immediately. Moreover, a man with administrative skill and managerial experience would be needed to organize the collection and storage effort.

Clearly, God had orchestrated Joseph's past experiences and trials for this moment. If his brothers had not sold him into slavery, he would not have been brought down to Egypt. If Potiphar had not purchased him from the slave market, he would not have gained the experience he needed to manage people and commodities within an Egyptian context. If he had not been falsely accused and sent to prison, he would not have interpreted the cupbearer's dream. And if that had not happened, he would not have been summoned by the Pharaoh on this divinely appointed day. His responsibilities in Potiphar's house and in the jailhouse had prepared him for his new role in Pharaoh's house. The Lord had overseen all those events to bring him to this one moment—when Joseph would be ready to organize a food drive of national proportions.

Because he had recognized God's hand on Joseph, the king immediately knew he should run the food-gathering operations.

And Pharaoh said to his servants, "Can we find such a one as this, a man in whom is the Spirit of God?" Then Pharaoh said to Joseph, "Inasmuch as God has shown you all this, there is no one as discerning and wise as you. You shall be over my house, and all my people shall be ruled according to your word; only in regard to the throne will I be greater than you." And Pharaoh said to Joseph, "See, I have set you over all the land of Egypt." (Genesis 41:38–41)

In a day, Joseph's fortunes had been completely reversed. That morning, he had awakened in his prison cell. By evening, he went to sleep in the palace. Thirteen years earlier, he had come to Egypt as a lowly slave, but now, at the age of thirty, he had become the second-most-powerful ruler in the land.

Undoubtedly, even at this time of exaltation, Joseph still wondered about his father and his brothers back in Canaan. What would they think if they could see him now? And what of the dreams God had given him when he was still at home? The Lord had revealed to him the meaning of other people's visions. But what about his own?

A FAMILY REUNION

The next seven years were years of abundance, and they passed quickly. During this time, Joseph was busy organizing the collection and storage of grain in all the cities throughout Egypt. His efforts were so successful that it became impossible to keep an accurate count of all the supply.

It was also during this time that Joseph got married and started a family. God's goodness to him is reflected in the names of his two sons. He called his oldest son *Manasseh*, which means *forgetful*, because as he put it, "God has made me forget all my toil and all my father's house" (Genesis 41:51). His younger son he named *Ephraim*, meaning *fruitful*. As Joseph himself explained, "For God has caused me to be fruitful in the land of my affliction" (v. 52). Despite all that Joseph had endured, God was still at the center of his thinking. The Lord enabled him to put the pain of his past behind him and to enjoy blessings in the very place where he had endured so many trials. Though Egypt was about to experience a great famine, Joseph was beginning to experience great abundance.

When the good years ended and the famine began, Joseph's diligent preparations paid off. Not only were the Egyptians themselves spared from mass starvation, but multitudes of people suffering famine in the surrounding nations came to Egypt to buy food. Joseph's foresight and careful planning saved the lives of millions of people throughout the middle-eastern world. It also greatly increased Pharaoh's wealth (Genesis 47:14–24).

Significantly, among those affected by the famine were the members of Joseph's family back in Canaan. Like everyone else, they eventually ran out of food and were forced to come to Egypt to purchase grain. As Jacob told his sons in Genesis 42:2, "Indeed I have heard that there is grain in Egypt; go down to that place and buy for us there, that we may live and not die." Twenty years after they sold their brother into slavery, Jacob's ten oldest sons made the same trek to Egypt that Joseph had been forced to make long ago.

God had allowed Joseph to endure so much so that, through his efforts, the family of Israel might be rescued from famine and brought to a place where they could grow into a large nation. It was all part of fulfilling the promise the Lord had made with Abraham three generations earlier (cf. Genesis 15:13–14). In an ironic turn of divine providence, Joseph's brothers came to Egypt in order to avoid death and would be rescued by the very person they had sought to kill two decades earlier.

When Joseph's brothers first appeared before him, they did not recognize him. He was twenty years older, clean-shaven, dressed as an Egyptian, and in a position of great authority. They would have assumed, if he were still alive, he was a slave somewhere. He also spoke to them through a translator. On the other hand, Joseph did recognize them. When they bowed before him, distant memories flooded his mind as he recalled the dreams of his youth (Genesis 42:6–9). But rather than immediately reveal his identity to them, Joseph decided first to test his brothers to see if their hearts had changed.

Through several interactions, over an extended period, Joseph created a scenario in which he would be able to observe their true character. During the first meeting, he told them not to return to

Egypt unless they brought their youngest brother, Benjamin, back with them. Many months later, they reluctantly returned with Benjamin. At the second meeting, Joseph secretly placed a silver goblet in Benjamin's bag so that when it was discovered as the brothers were returning to Canaan, Benjamin would be arrested for stealing. For his punishment, he would become a slave in Egypt while the other brothers would be allowed to go free.

Joseph watched to see how his brothers might respond. Would they give Benjamin up as a slave, like they had done with him? Would they think only about saving themselves and then concoct a story to explain to their father why Benjamin had not returned home with them? Or would they seek to save their younger brother—exposing themselves to prison to protect him?

Joseph's heart was certainly full when all his brothers returned with Benjamin, their robes torn in distress, and their voices appealing for his release. He was probably surprised, and delighted, when Judah—the brother who had first suggested selling Joseph as a slave—offered himself as a substitute for Benjamin's life. With earnest pleading, Judah said to Joseph, "Now therefore, please let your servant remain instead of the lad as a slave to my lord, and let the lad go up with his brothers" (Genesis 44:33). Clearly, these were not the same men who had betrayed Joseph so many years before.

When he observed the selfless loyalty of his brothers toward Benjamin, Joseph could no longer contain himself. After dismissing his servants, he began to weep so loudly that the Egyptians heard him crying from the other rooms of the house. Tearfully, he revealed his identity to his brothers: "I am Joseph."

Mixed emotions of immense relief and total dread all at once coursed through their veins. The brother they had sold into slavery was now a ruler of Egypt! The Genesis account expresses their utter astonishment and anxiety with these words, "His brothers could not answer him, for they were dismayed in his presence" (Genesis 45:3).

But Joseph was not interested in seeking revenge. He had seen the Lord's hand of providence in their earlier actions. He understood that God had used him to preserve his family and to bring them down to Egypt. Everything was according to the Lord's will. Listen to the God-centered theology that undergirded Joseph's thinking. In Genesis 45:4–8, he comforted his brothers with these words:

> I am Joseph your brother, whom you sold into Egypt. But now, do not therefore be grieved or angry with yourselves because you sold me here; for God sent me before you to preserve life. For these two years the famine has been in the land, and there are still five years in which there will be neither plowing nor harvesting. And God sent me before you to preserve a posterity for you in the earth, and to save your lives by a great deliverance. So now it was not you who sent me here, but God; and He has made me a father to Pharaoh, and lord of all his house, and a ruler throughout all the land of Egypt.

Three times, Joseph emphasized that God's hand was behind it all. Joseph was not excusing his brothers' sin, but he was emphasizing the fact that, in His sovereign purposes, the Lord even uses the wicked choices of sinful people to accomplish His desired ends. Because God sent Joseph to Egypt, Israel and his sons were saved from a famine that could have wiped out the family.

When Jacob heard the news that his son Joseph was still alive, he was so stunned that his heart momentarily stopped (Genesis 45:26). He was already 130 years old, but he eagerly readied himself for a journey to Egypt to see his favored son. As he travelled, God appeared to him in a vision and reiterated the fact that this was all part of His design to fulfill His covenant with Abraham. The Lord told Jacob, "I am God, the God of your father; do not fear to go down to Egypt, for I will make of you a great nation there" (Genesis 46:3; cf. 12:1–3).

Pharaoh gladly received Joseph's father and brothers and offered them the best land in Egypt—a region called Goshen. There, they were able to rear their families, raise their livestock, and thrive. Jacob's family, totaling seventy people, moved to Egypt after two years of the famine had passed (Genesis 45:6). Jacob lived another seventeen years in Egypt and died at the age of 147. Some four hundred fifty years later, they would become a nation of two million, ready to receive their promise back in the land of Canaan.

FORGIVENESS REITERATED

Joseph would have been fifty-six years old when his father died, and when his brothers bowed before him one more time—fearful that with Jacob's passing, Joseph might finally enact vengeance upon them. As Genesis 50:15 explains, "When Joseph's brothers saw that their father was dead, they said, 'Perhaps Joseph will hate us, and may actually repay us for all the evil which we did to him.'" Their hatred for Joseph had been real. But Joseph's hatred toward them existed only in their imaginations.

As we saw at the beginning of this chapter, Joseph was not interested in petty revenge. His trust in God's providential power outweighed any feelings of personal animosity toward his brothers. He recognized that everything that had happened to him was part of the Lord's perfect plan. Thus, he could tell his brothers, "As for you, you meant evil against me; but God meant it for good, in order to bring it about as it is this day, to save many people alive" (Genesis 50:20).

For Joseph, talking about God's sovereign providence was not an excuse for laziness or a cheap cliché; it was truly the theme of his life. He had been betrayed by his brothers, sold into slavery, falsely accused by his master's wife, wrongly incarcerated, and forgotten in prison. Yet through it all, the Lord blessed Joseph, and he learned to trust in the providential power of God (cf. Acts 7:9–14). He came to understand that God had a purpose in his suffering—and that through it, the Lord would save the Israelites and bring them to Egypt. Eventually, they would return to the land God had promised them. By faith, Joseph even affirmed that reality (cf. Hebrews 11:22).

Because of the way Joseph responded to his brothers, and because of the way he submitted himself to the will of God, biblical scholars have sometimes compared him to none other than the Lord Jesus Christ. Without overstating the case, there are some interesting parallels between the lives of Joseph and Jesus. For example, Joseph was dearly loved by his father and was a shepherd of his father's sheep. He was hated by his brothers, stripped of his robe, sold for the price of a slave, taken to Egypt, tempted, falsely accused, bound in chains, and condemned with criminals. Yet, after he suffered, he was highly exalted. He was thirty years old when he began his public service; he wept for his brothers, forgave those who had wronged him, and ultimately saved them from certain death. Moreover, what men did to hurt him, God turned around for good. All those things—albeit in a more profound and eternally significant sense—were also true of Jesus. Although the New Testament never specifically identifies Joseph as a type of Christ, certain aspects of Joseph's life seem to foreshadow the coming of Jesus.

PRACTICING A FAITH LIKE JOSEPH'S

Though Joseph's circumstances were unique to him, his perspective is one that all believers ought to emulate. The God who superintended the events of Genesis 37–50 still sits on the throne of the universe. He was sovereign over the circumstances of Joseph's life, and He is sovereign over our circumstances too. We may not always understand what is happening around us, but like Joseph, we can rest confidently in the fact that the Lord is in complete control.

Throughout the Scriptures, the theme of God's sovereignty is repeatedly presented as a comfort to believers. We need be anxious for nothing because our Heavenly Father reigns over all. He is all-powerful, all-wise, and all-present, and He has promised to work all things together for His glory and our good (Romans 8:28). We have nothing to fear because if God is for us, who can be against us? No one can oppose His will, and nothing can thwart His plans (Isaiah 14:27).

Consider some of the many ways in which God exercises His sovereign control:

- He is sovereign over everything (Job 42:2; Psalm 103:19, 115:3; Daniel 4:35, 7:13–14; Ephesians 1:11).
- He is sovereign over Satan and angels (Job 1:9–12; Psalm 103:20–21; Mark 1:27; Acts 10:38; Revelation 13:7).
- He is sovereign over the natural world (Job 37:10–14; Psalm 135:6–7; Matthew 5:45; 6:25–30; Mark 4:39).
- He is sovereign over history—past, present, and future (Isaiah 46:10; Daniel 2:21, 28).
- He is sovereign over the nations (2 Chronicles 20:6; Job 12:23; Psalm 22:28, 33:10–11, 47:7–9; Acts 17:26).
- He is sovereign over human rulers and governments (Ezra 1:1; Proverbs 21:1; Isaiah 40:23; Daniel 4:34–35; Romans 9:17).
- He is sovereign over the lives of men (1 Samuel 2:6–7; Psalm 139:16; Proverbs 16:9, 19:21; Lamentations 3:37; Galatians 1:15–16; James 4:15).
- He is sovereign over the animal world (1 Kings 17:4–6; Psalm 104:21–30; Jonah 1:17).
- He is sovereign over seeming chance and minute details (Proverbs 16:33; Jonah 1:7; Matthew 10:29–30).
- He is sovereign over the safekeeping of His children (Psalm 4:8, 5:12; Romans 8:28, 38–39).
- He is sovereign over personal needs (Matthew 10:29–31; Philippians 4:19).
- He is sovereign over calamity and trials (Ecclesiastes 7:14; Isaiah 45:7; Lamentations 3:38; Amos 3:6).

- He is sovereign over death and disease (Exodus 4:11; Deuteronomy 32:39).
- He is sovereign in answering prayer (Matthew 6:8; Philippians 4:6–7).
- He is sovereign over the wicked deeds of sinful men (Genesis 45:5–8, 50:20).
- He is sovereign in bringing the wicked to justice (Psalm 7:11–12; Proverbs 16:4; Romans 12:19).

The Scripture is explicit in its depiction of God's sovereign control over all things. In this chapter, we've considered just one illustration of His perfect providence—even in using the wicked actions of sinful people to accomplish His will. Joseph's example reminds us that "our God is in heaven; He does whatever He pleases" (Psalm 115:3). That means we can trust Him and wholly rest in the reality that He is on His throne. Embracing that kind of perspective won't take our trials away, but it will enable us to find joy and peace in the midst of them (James 1:3–5). Thus, even when others hurt us or life seems difficult and unfair, we can triumphantly declare with Joseph, "As for you, you meant evil against me; but God meant it for good."

3
MIRIAM: THE LEADING LADY OF THE EXODUS

For I brought you up from the land of Egypt,
I redeemed you from the house of bondage;
And I sent before you Moses, Aaron, and Miriam.

—MICAH 6:4

ACCORDING TO CENSUS DATA, the most common girl's name in the United States has historically been *Mary*. In fact, forms of *Mary* (or *Maria*) comprise the most popular girl's name in the Western world. This is due, of course, to the spiritual legacy of Jesus' mother Mary. Because of the notable way that she was used by God, more women have been named after her than anyone else.

But have you ever wondered whom Mary was named after? Here's a hint: the Greek rendering of her name is actually *Mariam*. Like many women throughout Jewish history, Mary was named for one of the most fascinating and unlikely heroines of the Old Testament.

Her namesake was none other than Moses' sister Miriam, a woman who was also used by God in a unique and noteworthy way.

Almost everyone has heard the story of Israel's exodus from Egypt—when God miraculously liberated His people from slavery. We all know about Moses, and even his brother Aaron, and we are familiar with their respective roles in that great deliverance. But how much do you know about their older sister, Miriam? The Bible depicts her as the leading lady of the Exodus. So what was her involvement in the most important redemptive event in Old Testament history?

SETTING THE STAGE

Three hundred fifty years is a long time by any measure. When we come to the opening chapters of Exodus, that is how long the Israelites have been living in the land of Egypt.

The book of Genesis ends with an account of the final days of Jacob and Joseph. As we saw in the previous chapter, God had exalted Joseph to a position of great prominence, and Joseph's family had been welcomed and shown favor by the Pharaoh. Even after Joseph died, the Hebrew people flourished and multiplied greatly—going from a family of seventy to a small nation numbering in the hundreds of thousands.

But by the time the narrative in Exodus begins, the situation has drastically changed. In the centuries that followed Joseph's death, "there arose a new king over Egypt, who did not know Joseph" (Exodus 1:8). Whether out of true ignorance or willful disregard, this new monarch did not care about the contributions Joseph had made generations earlier. His only concern, regarding the Israelites, was that their growing numbers posed a potential threat to his power. Thus, he told his people, "Look, the people of the children of Israel are more and mightier than we; come, let us deal shrewdly with them, lest they multiply, and it happen, in the event of war, that they also join our enemies and fight against us, and so go up out of the land" (Exodus 1:9–10). Pharaoh conspired against the descendants of Judah, who suddenly found themselves enslaved in Egypt.

Per Pharaoh's orders, the Egyptians assigned taskmasters over the Israelites, afflicting them with hard labor and making their lives miserable. But if the goal was to slow the growth of the Hebrew population, the Egyptian plan backfired because "the more they afflicted them, the more they multiplied and grew. And [the Egyptians] were in dread of the children of Israel" (Exodus 1:12).

As another new Pharaoh came to power, he was determined to find a more effective solution for dealing with the Israelites. Convinced that drastic times called for drastic measures, he conceived a new and brutal plan. His policy toward Hebrew baby boys was cruel and severe: "Every son who is born you shall cast into the river" (Exodus 1:22).

Pausing the narrative at this point, we turn to one family of those Hebrew slaves and a daughter named Miriam. This family, along with all the people of Israel, had been suffering under the oppressive burden of enslavement for many years. Then came the act of stunning cruelty, the imperial decree sentencing all newborn boys to death by drowning. The descendants of Jacob, in desperation, cried out to God for deliverance. Among them was a man named Amram, the father of Miriam and her younger brother, Aaron. For Amram, Pharaoh's new policy of murdering Hebrew babies was of very personal import. His wife, Jochebed, was pregnant with their third child. If the baby was a boy, he was to be killed on the day he was born.

That child was indeed a baby boy. We know him as Moses.

WELCOMING BABY MOSES

Jewish tradition indicates that while Moses was still in the womb, Miriam's father pleaded with the Lord to rescue the Hebrew people from the oppression they suffered in Egypt. According to Josephus, the first-century Jewish historian, God answered those prayers by appearing to Amram in a dream and promising that his newborn son would grow up to deliver all the Israelites from their bondage. The biblical record does not include those details, but Hebrews 11:23 does highlight the faith that characterized Amram and Jochebed: "By faith Moses, when he was born, was hidden three months by his parents, because they saw he was a beautiful child; and they were not afraid of the king's command." Because they trusted the Lord, Moses' parents refused to obey Pharaoh's merciless decree. They managed to keep their son's birth a secret, and they were determined to keep him hidden for as long as they could.

The author of Hebrews notes that Moses was a beautiful child, a point that is also made in Exodus 2:2. But that description includes more than just Moses' physical features. Acts 7:20 adds that baby Moses was "lovely in the sight of God" (NASB), a phrase that helps us understand the true nature of his handsome appearance. His parents understood that this child was fair in the eyes of the Lord— that is, that he had a divine destiny. So they trusted in God for his protection.

After three months had passed, his parents knew that they could no longer keep Moses hidden from the Egyptian authorities. So in an amazing act of faith, entrusting Moses to the Lord, they set him afloat in a basket on the Nile River. Speaking of Moses' mother, Exodus 2:3 explains what took place: "When she could no longer hide him, she took an ark of bulrushes for him, daubed it with asphalt and pitch, put the child in it, and laid it in the reeds by the river's bank." Significantly, the word *ark* in that verse (which some versions translate as *basket*) is the same Hebrew word used to refer to Noah's ark in Genesis 6–9. In fact, that's the only other place it occurs in the Old Testament. Just as Noah was spared by building an ark and covering it with pitch, so baby Moses was delivered from Pharaoh's edict by floating in an "ark" that was similarly covered with water-proof resin. Pharaoh's edict was that newborn Hebrew boys should be cast into the Nile. Ironically, the way Moses was placed into that very same river was the means of both his survival and the fulfilling of God's plan for him.

Undoubtedly, Moses' mother picked a spot on the Nile that would have been relatively safe for her newborn son. The fact that he was placed among the reeds suggests that he was near the shore, in the shade, and in a place where she hoped his tiny raft would not be carried away by the current. It is reasonable to assume that Moses' floating basket was strategically placed in an area where it would likely be discovered, probably near a royal bathing area. But who would find baby Moses, and what would they do with him? Those were details that only God could sovereignly orchestrate.

WATCHING BY THE RIVER

It is at this point in the Exodus account that our heroine enters the biblical narrative. As a young girl and the daughter of slaves, Miriam was certainly an unlikely hero. Yet she played a vital role in the life of her baby brother at this critical time in his life, when he was only three months old. We don't know exactly how old Miriam was at the time, yet God used her in a crucial way to accomplish His per-fect purposes for her brother—and ultimately for the nation of Israel. And this is only the beginning of her amazing story.

Miriam had heard the prayers of her father, observed the affec-tion of her mother towards Moses, and witnessed the faith of both in their protective defiance of Pharaoh's edict. Over the previous three months, she had naturally grown to love her baby brother and wanted to help protect him in any way she could. It is likely that she even helped her mother construct the waterproof basket in which

Moses set sail. And now she faced a great responsibility—to follow her baby brother as he floated in the Nile. Full of trepidation, she watched, hoping for the best.

The biblical account does not name the princess. Some scholars have suggested that perhaps this was Hatshepsut, who would eventually become Pharaoh herself and one of Egypt's most famous female rulers. But whoever she was, God used this princess to rescue Moses from the river and to make it possible for him to be trained in all aspects of Egyptian learning and culture—an education that would prove invaluable for Moses' later role as Israel's deliverer.

According to Josephus, the princess called for several Egyptian nursemaids to try to comfort baby Moses, but he just continued crying. So Miriam bravely closed the safe distance and, approaching Pharaoh's daughter without identifying herself, suggested that perhaps a Hebrew nursemaid might have some success in comforting the baby. In a shrewd and bold action, she asked, "Shall I go and call a nurse for you from the Hebrew women, that she may nurse the child for you?" (Exodus 2:7).

The princess agreed, and Miriam's strategy unfolded as she went to find her mother. When Jochebed arrived, "Pharaoh's daughter said to her, 'Take this child away and nurse him for me, and I will give you your wages.' So the woman took the child and nursed him" (Exodus 2:9). Once again, God's providence brought about a remarkable result. Miriam's courage led to Moses' mother being paid to raise her own son! She could do so at home, and without any fear of the Egyptian authorities.

It is likely that Moses lived with his birth family until he was nine or ten years old, and maybe even until he was twelve. During those formative years, he would have been taught about the true God and about his forefathers, Abraham, Isaac, and Jacob. He would have identified with his people and learned that God had called him to be their deliverer. The Lord would use this early training to shape Moses' character and convictions so that later in his life, he would refuse "to be called the son of Pharaoh's daughter, choosing rather to suffer affliction with the people of God than to enjoy the passing pleasures of sin" (Hebrews 11:24–25).

When Moses had grown and become a young man, he was brought to the princess and legally adopted by her (Exodus 2:10). He was then given a royal education and became "learned in all the wisdom of the Egyptians" (Acts 7:22). His formal education would have included instruction in reading, writing, arithmetic, and perhaps one or more of the languages of Canaan. He would also have participated in various outdoor sports such as archery and horseback riding. In all of this, God was preparing Moses with skills he would use to lead the Israelites out of Egypt.

At the very beginning of Moses' life, the Lord used his older sister, Miriam, in a specific way, to watch over him and bring him safely back home. In her willingness to bravely approach Pharaoh's daughter, Miriam played a strategic role in her baby brother's return to his family. She was emboldened by the faith she had seen in her parents, and which she herself possessed. Moreover, in watching the Lord rescue Moses from the Nile River, Miriam herself was being prepared for the day when she would see God deliver her people from their bondage in Egypt.

WAITING FOR DELIVERANCE

During those years, Miriam shared family life with her baby brother as he grew into a young boy. Her other brother, Aaron, was three years older than Moses. Together, the three children were taught about God and their family history and also instructed concerning their future. Moses, in particular, would have been reminded that the Lord had unique plans for his life. All three children would one day be used by God together in Israel's exodus from Egypt.

When the day came for Moses to leave for the palace, Miriam

was no doubt there to say goodbye. She had watched Moses' floating basket from afar when he was but a baby; in a similar way, she continued to observe him from a distance as he grew into adulthood—not as the son of slaves but as an adopted prince of Egypt. As she watched and waited, she would surely have wondered when God would elevate Moses to deliver her enslaved people from Egypt.

The biblical account does not tell us much about what Moses did during his days as an Egyptian prince. Acts 7:22 simply states that, in addition to being well-educated, he "was mighty in words and deeds." But even as a prince, he never forgot where he came from. According to Josephus, Moses continued to identify with the Hebrew people to the point that many of the Egyptians became suspicious of him and even looked for opportunities to kill him.

On one occasion, after the neighboring Ethiopians attacked Egypt, Pharaoh made Moses a general in his army and sent him to fight the invaders. As Josephus tells the story, Pharaoh saw this as a win-win situation. If Moses succeeded, the Ethiopians would be driven out of the land. But if Moses failed, he would likely be killed, and the threat he represented would be eliminated. Once again, the Egyptian plan did not have its desired effect. Due to some brilliant strategizing by the young general, Moses' military campaign was a smashing success—so much so that when he returned home, the Egyptian nobles were more afraid of him than before.

The biblical narrative picks up the story when Moses was forty years old. Having identified himself with his native people, Moses:

. . . went out to his brethren and looked at their burdens. And he saw an Egyptian beating a Hebrew, one of his brethren. So he looked this way and that way, and when he saw no one, he killed the Egyptian and hid him in the sand. And when he went out the second day, behold, two Hebrew men were fighting, and he said to the one who did the wrong, "Why are you striking your companion?" Then he said, "Who made you a prince and a judge over us?

Do you intend to kill me as you killed the Egyptian?" So Moses feared and said, "Surely this thing is known!" (Exodus 2:11–14).

Acts 7:25 explains the motivation behind Moses' seemingly reckless actions. Apparently, he was already eager to deliver Israel, "for he supposed that his brethren would have understood that God would deliver them by his hand, but they did not understand." Clearly, it was not yet God's time, and Moses' act of violence—in killing the Egyptian taskmaster—cannot be condoned. Nonetheless, his zeal was evidence of his profound identification with the people of God and his total rejection of everything that Egypt had to offer (cf. Hebrews 11:24–26).

When Pharaoh heard what Moses had done, he sought to kill him. If the Egyptians had already been suspicious of Moses, this event clearly confirmed their worst fears. Running for his life, Moses fled to Midian—the place where he would spend the next four decades of his life tending sheep and being humbled and shaped by God.

Through all of this Miriam was waiting as her brother rose to a position of prominence and then fled in disgrace as a fugitive. Josephus tells us that she was married to Hur, a descendant of Judah, and that together they had a family. Just as Miriam and her two brothers had been instructed by their parents, now she instilled within her children a longing and hope for divine deliverance.

Moses was forty years old when he left Egypt, and he spent another forty years in Midian—meaning that he was eighty years old when he finally returned (Exodus 7:7). For eight long decades, Miriam had waited. She had always known that Moses was God's chosen deliverer; yet she did not know when that deliverance would begin. When the Pharaoh who banished Moses died (Exodus 2:23–25), her hope must have begun to mount. Surely her heart raced when Aaron reported to her that God had told him to go meet Moses in the wilderness (Exodus 4:27).

Undoubtedly, Miriam's excitement only grew when her brothers first confronted Pharaoh and then with each successive plague. Perhaps she remembered watching Moses float down the Nile, even as she witnessed the water of Egypt's mighty river turn to blood (Exodus 7:20–21). As frogs, flies, lice, boils, hail, and locusts afflicted the Egyptians, Miriam and her fellow Hebrews—protected by God in Goshen—must have been filled with awe and a growing realization that the Lord had finally heard their cries (Exodus 3:7), and their redemption from bondage was at hand.

Miriam and her family would have participated in the first Passover (Exodus 12:1–28). They would have killed a lamb and painted its blood on the doorposts of their house just as Moses instructed them. And they would have eaten the meat and prepared themselves to leave Egypt in haste. They would have been kept safe as God's judgment by the angel of death was handed out in the slaughter of all the firstborn sons of Egypt.

It is difficult to imagine the jubilee that reverberated throughout the Hebrew ranks as they were awakened early that next morning with the news that it was time to leave. They had been in Egypt a total of 430 years (Exodus 12:41), and at last the Lord was leading them out. Though Pharaoh had continually rebuffed the pleas of Moses and Aaron, in spite of the miraculous plagues that God had brought, he finally relented and insisted that the Israelites should leave. After many lifetimes of waiting, in fulfillment of divine promises that were centuries old, Miriam and her people were being set free.

WORSHIPPING ON THE SHORE

Not surprisingly, given his track record, Pharaoh changed his mind only a few days after the Israelites began their journey out of Egypt. According to Exodus 14:5, "the heart of Pharaoh and his servants was turned against the people; and they said, 'Why have we done this, that we have let Israel go from serving us?'" The hard-hearted king summoned his army and gave chase to his former slaves.

The massive company of Hebrews, of whom there were six hundred thousand men plus women and children (Exodus 12:37), moved slowly but methodically—following the Lord's direction as He led them with a pillar of cloud by day and a pillar of fire by night (Exodus 13:21). But the Egyptian army soon caught up with them. Josephus reports that in addition to six hundred select chariots (Exodus 14:7), Pharaoh's army consisted of fifty thousand horsemen and two hundred thousand foot soldiers. With their backs to the Red Sea, the people of Israel began to panic. With very short memories of the miraculous signs and amazing deliverance just experienced in Egypt, they complained against Moses for leading them out in the first place, saying, "Because there were no graves in Egypt, have you taken us away to die in the wilderness? . . . For it would have been better for us to serve the Egyptians than that we should die in the wilderness" (Exodus 14:11–12).

From the human perspective the situation certainly looked grim. The Israelites, unarmed and untrained, were not ready for any battle. Against them stood one of the most advanced and efficient armies of the ancient world: hundreds of chariots, thousands of cavalry, and hundreds of thousands of infantry. And they were absolutely trapped against the Red Sea with nowhere to flee. The situation was hopeless, and the people reacted in hysteric desperation.

But Moses knew better. In the face of impossible circumstances, he trusted in the promises of the One who always does as He wills. His response to the people was charged with faith in the Lord: "Do not be afraid. Stand still, and see the salvation of the LORD, which He will accomplish for you today. For the Egyptians whom you see today, you shall see again no more forever. The LORD will fight for you, and you shall hold your peace" (Exodus 14:13–14).

What happened next has become one of the greatest Sunday school classics of all time. But we must not allow our familiarity with the story to take away from the remarkable nature of what happened. God moved the pillar of cloud between the Hebrew camp and the Egyptian camp—keeping the pursuing army in the dark while He provided a supernatural escape route for His people. Then as Moses stretched out his hand over the sea, the Lord sent a strong wind that separated the waters to provide a path of dry land right through the middle for the Israelites to traverse.

The parting of the Red Sea is surely one of the most well-known of all the biblical miracles, and in some ways, such familiarity may blunt the reality of the massive power and order of the divine event. This is not a cataclysm like those computer-generated in a fantasy film. This happened! And we already know God works very well with all forms of H_2O—just think back to Creation (Genesis 1:1–7) and the Flood (Genesis 6–9).

What actually took place is absolutely mind-boggling: to think that an ocean of water split in two and a dry road appeared down the middle! Vast walls of water, hundreds of feet high on either side and miles across from shore to shore, flanked the Israelites' escape route as they fled to safety on the far shore. Since this is easy for God, the biblical description of this astonishing event is surprisingly matter-of-fact. Exodus 14:21–22 simply states, "The LORD caused the sea to go back by a strong east wind all that night, and made the sea into dry land, and the waters were divided. So the children of Israel went into the midst of the sea on the dry ground, and the waters were a wall to them on their right hand and on their left." In a most unexpected and unpredictable way, the Lord had turned the people's terror into triumph.

As the Hebrew people were about to reach the other side, the Lord lifted the cloud, and the Egyptians realized they were escaping. Apparently the recent deadly plague miracles that killed so many of Israel's enemies in Egypt did not prove educational to the commanders or the troops because they immediately gave chase, in what would prove to be one of the most disastrous military decisions ever made. As the Egyptians made their way through the sea, God caused them to become confused and their chariots difficult to navigate. The pursuers, realizing they had made a deadly mistake, began to panic, "Let us flee from the face of Israel, for the LORD fights for them against the Egyptians" (Exodus 14:25). Talk about bad timing for clear thinking! As if being trapped in the valley between mountains of water and in total chaos were not enough, their escape was further hindered by the arrival of a sudden and severe thunderstorm (Psalm 77:17–19).

By this time, the Israelites had all arrived safely on the other shore. At that moment, God commanded Moses to once again stretch out his hand over the sea. As he did, the walls of water crashed together with a violence never occurring in any ordinary sea. In one catastrophic holocaust, the waters returned to their normal level to bury the mighty and massive army of Egypt like drowned rats. "The waters returned and covered the chariots, the horsemen, and all the army of Pharaoh that came into the sea after them. Not so much as one of them remained" (Exodus 14:28).

The Lord had rescued His people. And as they stood there on the shore, watching the smashing and drowning destruction of their enemies, the former slaves were awestruck. Exodus 14:31 says that they feared the Lord and believed in Him. Based on what had just happened, no other response would have been appropriate. Moses had earlier told them that the Lord would fight for them while they watched in silence (Exodus 14:14). There they stood safe and dry, speechless with astonishment, eyewitnesses to the supernatural power of their God.

When they could recover from the silent shock, they all burst out in song with a beautiful hymn of praise. That hymn, called the Song of Moses (Exodus 15:1–18), extols the power, glory, and supremacy of God. The words declare that there is no one like the God of Israel. Thus, they sang, "Who is like You, O LORD, among the gods? Who is like You, glorious in holiness, fearful in praises, doing wonders?"

(v. 11). The final line of their hymn summarized the heart of their worship: "The LORD shall reign forever and ever!" (v. 18).

It is in the midst of this stunned, jubilant praise that Miriam again appears. She, of course, had been there all along. She had seen the pillar of cloud every day and the pillar of fire every night. She had watched the Egyptian army approaching from a distance and felt the anxiety and panic of her people. She had also heard her brother's words of confident trust in God's promise and power. And she had walked with the rest in amazement through the sea. Hebrews 11:29 notes that it was "by faith they passed through the Red Sea as by dry land." They had to trust God that the mountains of seawater would not collapse on them. That was pure faith because no one had ever experienced any phenomenon like that before. Miriam lived her entire life with the confident expectation that God would deliver Israel, using her brother Moses. Time and again she had seen God's incredible power on display. But this had no equal. The Israelites had witnessed the Lord's might and faithfulness, but never in such an astonishing way.

In response to Moses' hymn, Miriam led the women of Israel in a joyous refrain of praise. Exodus 15:20–21 summarizes her joyful response with these words: "Then Miriam the prophetess, the sister of Aaron [and Moses], took the timbrel in her hand; and all the women went out after her with timbrels and with dances. And Miriam answered them: 'Sing to the LORD, for He has triumphed gloriously! The horse and its rider He has thrown into the sea!'"

These brief comments give us several fascinating insights into the woman Miriam had become. First, she is called a *prophetess*—one to whom God revealed messages for the people (cf. Numbers 12:2). She is the first woman in the Bible to be given that rare privilege. In the entire Old Testament, only three other women were referred to in this way—Deborah (Judges 4:4), Huldah (2 Kings 22:14), and Isaiah's wife (Isaiah 8:3). Second, her mention in Exodus 15 over any other person, male or female, suggests that she played a strategic role (along with both her brothers Moses and Aaron) in the events of the Exodus. The Lord Himself, speaking through the prophet Micah, noted her prominence when He said to Israel, "For I brought you up from the land of Egypt, I redeemed you from the house of bondage; and I sent before you Moses, Aaron, and Miriam" (Micah 6:4). In Exodus 15, we see her leadership displayed with particular reference to the women of Israel, as the women followed her in singing.

Third, and perhaps most significantly, these verses give us a glimpse into Miriam's soul—as one who worshipped the Lord with heartfelt emotion. Like the song of Moses that preceded it, Miriam's song centered on the power and glory of God. She worshipped not only in word and melody, but also with instruments and dancing. And she led others to join with her in exuberance and thanksgiving, setting a precedent for later generations of Israelite women (cf. 1 Samuel 18:6). Eighty years earlier, Miriam had watched the Lord providentially deliver Moses from the waters of the Nile River into the care of Pharaoh's family. On this day, she again experienced God's hand of deliverance—as He rescued His people from the waters of the Red Sea and out of the hands of Pharaoh's army. In both cases, the water spelled death. And in both cases, God demonstrated His unsurpassed power and unfailing faithfulness to His people and His promise.

WEAKNESS IN THE WILDERNESS

With epic visions of the Red Sea experience carved into their minds, the Israelites traveled through the desert toward Mount Sinai. If the power of God is amazing, so is the weakness of people! Even in fresh memory of God's great power, the people soon began to complain. When they arrived at Marah, they grumbled because the only water they could find was bitter and unpalatable. God graciously transformed the water so that it became drinkable (Exodus 15:25). In the Wilderness of Sin the people complained that they had no food; in response, the Lord provided both manna and quail (Exodus 16:4, 13). At Rephidim, when again there was no water, the forgetful and faithless Israelites became angry. Again, even with their unbelief, the Lord provided. He instructed Moses to strike a rock with his staff and water poured out for the people to drink (Exodus 17:6).

Despite their grumbling, God continued to preserve and protect His people. When the Amalekites attacked them, God gave Israel the victory in an extraordinary way. While Joshua led Israel's troops into battle, Moses stood on a hilltop with Aaron and Hur. "And so it was, when Moses held up his hand, that Israel prevailed; and when he let down his hand, Amalek prevailed. But Moses' hands became heavy; so they took a stone and put it under him, and he sat on it. And Aaron and Hur supported his hands, one on one side, and the other on the other side; and his hands were steady until the going down of the sun" (Exodus 17:11–12). We have already noted that, according to Josephus, Hur was Miriam's husband. That would mean that Moses' hands were supported by his brother, Aaron, on one side, and by his brother-in-law, Hur, on the other.

All of this took place in the first two months of their journey out of Egypt, before the Israelites arrived at Mount Sinai on the first day of the third month (Exodus 19:1). The rest of the book of Exodus details their stay at Sinai, where God gave them His law, including the Ten Commandments, and the instructions for building the Tabernacle. Of special note, with regard to Miriam, is that God selected a man named Bezalel as a craftsman for the Tabernacle. Exodus 35:30 explains that this man was the grandson of Hur; so Miriam would have been Bezalel's grandmother. According to rabbinic tradition, the Lord blessed Miriam with such an illustrious descendant because she had been faithful to obey God, and not Pharaoh, back in Egypt.

The Israelites stayed at Sinai for eleven months before resuming their journey (Numbers 10:11). Almost as soon as they left, the people began to grumble and complain—much like they had done before they had arrived at Sinai. In response to their murmuring, the Lord judged them with both fire and plague (Numbers 11:1, 33). Even before they had left Sinai, the Israelites had grown impatient with Moses and built the infamous golden calf in his absence (Exodus 32). The result was that the Lord's anger burned against their idolatry and thousands of them were killed.

As members of Moses' family, Miriam and Aaron would have been constantly exposed to the complaints of the people. (In Exodus 32:22–23, Aaron even blamed the mobbing crowds for pressuring him into casting the golden calf.) Evidently, those voices of protest began to have a poisonous effect on their thinking. Even though they had witnessed God's repeated judgment against those who grumbled, Moses' siblings unexpectedly joined in the dissension and became disloyal to their brother. In Numbers 12, the story of Miriam turns ugly.

Apparently resentful of their younger brother, Miriam and Aaron criticized him for having married a non-Jewish woman (v. 1). But that was not really the reason for their protest. In verse 2, their acidic questions exposed their true motive—jealousy: "Has the LORD indeed spoken only through Moses? Has He not spoken through us also?" Out of green envy, they openly challenged Moses' authority.

That kind of disloyalty might have been expected from the multitudes. But for it to gain a foothold in the thinking of Aaron and Miriam, especially, made it deeply toxic. The Lord's response came swiftly. Having summoned Moses, Aaron, and Miriam to the tent of meeting, the Lord said to them: "Hear now My words: If there is a prophet among you, I, the LORD, make Myself known to him in a vision; I speak to him in a dream. Not so with My servant Moses; He is faithful in all My house. I speak with him face to face, even plainly, and not in dark sayings; and he sees the form of the LORD. Why then were you not afraid to speak against My servant Moses?" (Numbers 12:6–8). If there had been any question about Moses' position as God's appointed spokesman and leader, it vanished in that instant.

As the Lord departed from the tent, "suddenly Miriam became leprous, as white as snow. Then Aaron turned toward Miriam, and there she was, a leper" (v. 10). In shock and dismay, Aaron acknowledged their sin and begged Moses to intercede on his sister's behalf. The implication is that Miriam, too, responded in repentant sorrow. It is likely that she had instigated the attack on Moses, which is why she alone was given leprosy. In any case, Moses interceded for his sister and the Lord mercifully healed her. But in keeping with the laws of ceremonial cleansing, she was required to live outside the camp for seven days (v. 15). During that time, the Israelites waited for her before continuing on their journey, indicating that the entire nation was aware of what had happened.

The story of Miriam is suspended at the point of her healing and nothing more is revealed about her until her death. The silence suggests that, from this point on, Miriam submissively supported her brother Moses in his God-given role. In a moment of sinful weakness, she had challenged his authority. Perhaps it was hard for her, as the older sister who had watched over his cradle, to always submit herself to his leadership. But whatever her compulsions, the Lord made it clear what her attitude toward Moses had to be. The implication of the text is that she obeyed.

In the very next chapter, Numbers 13, the Israelites sent men to spy out the land of Canaan. When ten of the spies brought back a bad report, the people refused to trust God, and like a host of jealous siblings rebelled against Moses (Numbers 14:1–10). They obviously had not learned from Miriam's experience. As a result, the Lord sentenced them to forty years of wandering in the wilderness. The price of such disloyalty, against the Lord and His appointed servant, was very high. That faithless generation would not be allowed to enter the Promised Land, for which they had long waited. Their hope would die with them in the wilderness. They would never leave the barren places. God's promise would be fulfilled only for their children (Numbers 14:29–31).

According to Jewish tradition, Miriam's death did not come until the first month of the fortieth year of wilderness wandering. Numbers 20:1 gives this brief account, "Then the children of Israel, the whole congregation, came into the Wilderness of Zin in the first month, and the people stayed in Kadesh; and Miriam died there and was buried there." Josephus records in his history that the people celebrated her death with a public funeral followed by thirty days of mourning.

Both of Miriam's brothers would die that same year. Miriam had died in the first month, Aaron would follow in the fifth (Numbers 33:38), and Moses in the eleventh (Deuteronomy 1:3; 34:7). With the death of these three, the first generation passed away. The second generation of Israelites was now ready to enter the land under the leadership of Joshua.

MIRIAM'S LEGACY

Though they were not permitted to enter the Promised Land, these three siblings played an instrumental role in Israel's deliverance from Egypt—Moses as God's uniquely appointed deliverer; Aaron as Israel's first high priest; and Miriam as the leading lady of the Exodus.

As a young slave girl, she had watched over her baby brother when he floated in the Nile. As a wife and mother, she had waited in Egypt for deliverance to come. As an elderly woman, probably in her nineties, she had seen the power of God at the Red Sea, and she led the women of Israel in joyful celebration as a result. God used her husband Hur to help secure Israel's victory over the Amalekites, and He used her grandson Bezalel to help construct the Tabernacle. Though she sinfully challenged Moses' authority in the wilderness—and was severely rebuked as a result—she lived out the last four decades of her life submissively supporting Moses' authority. And when she died, the people of Israel mourned her passing for a full month, just as they mourned the deaths of Aaron (Numbers 20:29) and Moses (Deuteronomy 34:8). It's no wonder God included her name, along with those of her brothers, in Micah 6:4 when He said of the Exodus, "I sent before you Moses, Aaron, and Miriam."

Miriam's legacy is perhaps best seen in the fact that in later generations, hers became one of the most popular names for Jewish girls—especially during the time of Christ. In the New Testament there are at least six different women who bear the Greek form of her name ("Mariam" or "Maria"), which in English is translated as "Mary." These include Mary, the mother of Jesus; Mary Magdalene; Mary of Bethany, the sister of Martha and Lazarus; Mary, the mother of James and Joses; Mary, the mother of John Mark; and Mary of Rome (mentioned in Romans 16:6).

Of these New Testament women, commentators have sometimes drawn parallels between Mary the mother of Jesus and Miriam the sister of Moses. We should be careful not to overstate the similarities; however, both women were connected to great deliverers—Miriam to Moses, the foremost human deliverer of the Old Testament, and Mary to Jesus, the Messiah Himself. Both women watched over these deliverers when, as infants, their lives were endangered by wicked kings (Exodus 1:22; Matthew 2:16). Both women sang songs of praise to God in response to His deliverance—Miriam in Exodus 15:20–21 and Mary in Luke 1:46–55. And God used both women in the unfolding of His plan of redemption. Miriam was privileged to look after her baby brother, the one whom God used to redeem Israel from Egypt in a physical sense. And Mary was blessed to give birth to a baby boy, the One who would redeem the world from sin.

Miriam is rightly regarded as a hero, not because of her own greatness, but because she rested in faith on the mighty power of God. After eighty years of waiting in Egypt, her faith was rewarded and her hope realized. Though her life was notable on many fronts—as the sister of Moses and Aaron, the prophetess of Israel, the wife of Hur, and the grandmother of Bezalel—her greatest triumphs came when her heart was centered on the glory of God. As she herself sang on the shores of the Red Sea, "Sing to the LORD, for He has triumphed gloriously!" That refrain not only summarizes all that Miriam experienced in her life, including the events of the Exodus, but rightly stands as the theme of all human history.

4

GIDEON AND SAMSON: STORIES
OF WEAKNESS AND STRENGTH

~~~T~~~

*And what more shall I say? For the time would fail me to tell of Gideon
and Barak and Samson . . . who through faith subdued kingdoms,
worked righteousness, obtained promises, stopped the mouths of lions,
quenched the violence of fire, escaped the edge of the sword, [and] out of
weakness were made strong.*

—HEBREWS 11:32–34A

F OR US, THE WORD *JUDGE* IMMEDIATELY CONJURES IMAGES
of the courtroom. Whether it's the U.S. Supreme Court, with
its nine distinguished justices, or any of the thousands of lower
courts scattered across our country—a judge is a primary fixture on
a bench with a highly defined jurisdiction within the American legal
system. In our day, a judge wears a robe, wields a gavel, and presides
over a court of law. The judge instructs juries, hears cases, and ensures
that defendants receive the fair trial they've been promised by our
nation's Constitution.

But that is nothing at all like the judges in the biblical book of
Judges. In Old Testament Israel, after the time of Moses and Joshua

but before the reigns of Saul and David, the Israelites were protected, preserved, and ruled by a series of judges. This kind of *judge* was a deliverer—a defender of Israel raised up by God from among the people to rescue them from their enemies. Like modern justices, the judges of ancient Israel did on occasion make legal decisions that affected large numbers of people. But they were more like action figures. Rather than being legal experts, the judges of ancient Israel were primarily known for their military prowess, as they were armed to lead their people into battle. The Hebrew term, which can be rendered *judge*, also means *savior* or *deliverer*, and it is in that latter sense that the term applies to these unlikely heroes in Israel's history. They were both warriors and governors—who sought to protect and ensure freedom for their countrymen under the redemptive promises of God. For nearly three hundred fifty years in Israel's history, these saviors played a critical role in God's interaction with and protection of His chosen people.

FROM JOSHUA TO THE JUDGES

The book of Joshua ends with the Israelites, who have just entered the Promised Land, pledging to wholeheartedly honor the Lord. In Joshua 24:24, "the people said to Joshua, 'The LORD our God we will serve, and His voice we will obey!'" Years earlier, Moses had instructed the people that if they served the Lord faithfully, they would be blessed, but if they rebelled against God, they would be severely punished:

> See, I have set before you today life and good, death and evil, in that I command you today to love the LORD your God, to walk in His ways, and to keep His commandments, His statutes, and His judgments, that you may live and multiply; and the LORD your God will bless you in the land which you go to possess. But if

your heart turns away so that you do not hear, and are drawn away, and worship other gods and serve them, I announce to you today that you shall surely perish; you shall not prolong your days in the land which you cross over the Jordan to go in and possess. (Deuteronomy 30:15–18)

The people initially heeded the words of Moses. According to Judges 2:7, the generation of Joshua served the Lord faithfully. But shortly after they died off, another generation arose that committed the ultimate evil in God's sight by worshipping idols. Their spiritual infidelity was largely due to the fact that they had failed to drive the idolatrous Canaanites completely out of the Promised Land as God had commanded for their spiritual protection. The Israelites were continually tempted by the idolatry and immorality of their pagan neighbors (cf. Judges 1:28; 2:1–5).

The book of Judges records centuries of Israel's repeated spiritual failure and God's continual grace toward His rebellious people. The old adage that history repeats itself is especially evident during this time in Israel's past—where a cycle of rebellion, punishment, and deliverance recurred at least seven different times. Over and over, Israel fell away from the Lord and He punished them by allowing their enemies to oppress them. In desperation, the distraught Israelites would cry out to God for help, and He would graciously raise up a human judge to deliver His people (Judges 2:18). Then there would follow a time of peace—until a new generation forgot the Lord and the cycle was repeated.

During these four centuries, God appointed at least fourteen judges—at different times and in different regions. That appointment was not theirs by inheritance, popular vote, conquest, or man-made selection. Nor were the judges limited to a specific area or term. They were divinely random choices on the surface, but sovereignly placed in God's chosen cause.

The judges of God's choice include Othniel, Ehud, Shamgar,

Deborah (accompanied by Barak), Gideon, Tola, Jair, Jephthah, Ibzan, Elon, Abdon, Samson, Eli, and Samuel. By raising up these human deliverers, the Lord demonstrated His faithfulness to His covenant with Abraham and His power to fulfill it, even in the most dramatic fashion. His compassion and grace shone brightly against the dark backdrop of pitiful human compromise and twisted acts of sin. The final verses of Judges sum up the spiritual confusion that characterized Israel at this time: "In those days there was no king in Israel; everyone did what was right in his own eyes" (Judges 21:25).

In Israel's history, no group of heroes is more *unlikely* than the judges of the Old Testament. The chaotic nature of the time period combined with the unique (and sometimes uncivilized) individuals whom God chose to lead His people resulted in scenarios that were often complex and even bizarre. Nowhere is that seen more clearly than in the lives of the two men we will consider in this chapter. Gideon and Samson were both men with serious faults and would have been rejected by wise men from any critical duty of leadership. Yet the Lord chose them to sustain His people and to fulfill His redemptive purpose. Their weaknesses only serve to highlight God's infinite power—which triumphed through them in spite of their imperfections.

Let's begin by looking at God's strength displayed in the life of a deliverer named Gideon.

GIDEON: A WEAK MAN MADE STRONG

The account of Gideon begins in Judges 6. From the outset, he is depicted as a man whose fear was greater than his faith. The same was true of his fellow countrymen. For seven years, they had lived in perpetual dread of the bordering Midianites and Amalekites, who repeatedly raided Israel's land, destroying their crops and stealing their livestock. Weary of hiding in caves in the mountains, the Israelites finally cried out to the Lord for help.

THE LEADER WHO LACKED COURAGE

That the Lord selected Gideon as the answer to deliver Israel is proof that His power cannot be limited even by the most unlikely human instrument. When we first meet Gideon, he is hiding from the Midianites—attempting to covertly thresh wheat in a winepress (Judges 6:11). The process of beating out grain and separating it from the chaff normally took place out in the open, on a hilltop, where the breeze would blow the chaff away. But fearful that enemy marauders might spot him, Gideon took cover in the quarried shelter of a winepress. The location was far from ideal for winnowing wheat, but at least his efforts would go undetected, or so he imagined.

As Gideon worked his humdrum task with fearful fervency, an astonishing event happened—the Angel of the Lord suddenly appeared to him. The evidence in the Old Testament of such appearances indicates that the Angel appeared in a form like a man, and that is why there is no shock and panic as might occur if the appearance were of heavenly glory. Gideon did not fall into a traumatic sleep like those who actually saw the glory of God (such as Isaiah, Ezekiel, John, and Paul). Instead, he carried on a conversation.

No doubt what startled him was the reality that his hiding place had been discovered. But Gideon would have been even more surprised to hear the Angel speak to him and say, "The LORD is with you, you mighty man of valor!" (v. 12). From Gideon's perspective, both parts of that greeting were questionable. "If the LORD is with us, why then has all this happened to us?" he asked in verse 13. "And where are all His miracles which our fathers told us about, saying, 'Did not the Lord bring us up from Egypt?' But now the LORD has forsaken us and delivered us into the hands of the Midianites." Driven by doubt, Gideon went on to deny that he was a man of bravery: "O my Lord, how can I save Israel? Indeed my clan is the weakest in Manasseh, and I am the least in my father's house" (v. 15). Clearly, faith and fortitude were qualities Gideon sorely lacked.

Yet in calling him a man of valor, the Angel of the Lord was not referring to what Gideon was, but what he would become by the strength that God provided. Thus, He said to Gideon, "Surely I will be with you, and you shall defeat the Midianites as one man" (v. 16). When the Lord came upon him, this faithless coward would accomplish incredible feats of bravery in delivering Israel. Gideon was so skeptical that such a possibility could come from a doubting coward like him that he demanded a sign from God. The Lord graciously consented. When the faithless farmer offered bread and meat to his heavenly visitor, He miraculously consumed it with fire before disappearing from his sight (v. 21).

It is important to note that the Angel of the Lord is identified in Judges 6 as the Lord Himself (vv. 14, 16, 23, 25, 27). That is why He gladly accepted Gideon's offering of worship (vv. 18–21)—something an ordinary angel would never do (cf. Revelation 22:8–9). When Gideon finally realized that it was the Lord Himself he had seen, he was certain he would die.

> Now Gideon perceived that He was the Angel of the LORD. So Gideon said, "Alas, O LORD God! For I have seen the Angel of the Lord face to face." Then the LORD said to him, "Peace be with you; do not fear, you shall not die." (Judges 6:22–23)

The weight of biblical evidence indicates that the Angel of the Lord was the pre-incarnate Christ, the Second Member of the Trinity, appearing in bodily form—as He did on a number of occasions throughout the Old Testament era (cf. Genesis 16:7–14; 22:11–14; 31:11–13; Exodus 3:2–5; Numbers 22:22–35; Joshua 5:13–15; 1 Kings 19:5–7). The Angel's appearances throughout Israel's history, along with passages like Isaiah 9:6 and Daniel 7:13, provide strong Old Testament evidence for the deity of Jesus Christ.

That night, the Lord came to Gideon and instructed him to tear down an altar to Baal that was near his father's house. The young man obeyed, though with great trepidation. According to Judges

6:27, "Gideon took ten men from among his servants and did as the LORD had said to him. But because he feared his father's household and the men of the city too much to do it by day, he did it by night." Again, courage was not a familiar virtue to Gideon. Nonetheless, he had shown a willingness to obey the Lord, and that was progress in his faith.

THE STRATEGY THAT SEEMED SUICIDAL

When he heard that the Midianite invaders had returned, Gideon summoned the men of Israel to fight. In a remarkable display of valorous volunteerism, some thirty-two thousand warriors responded. But even with such a sizeable force under his command, Gideon doubted that he was the right person to lead them into battle. Once again, his faith was faltering, so he demanded another sign that God would be with him.

> So Gideon said to God, "If You will save Israel by my hand as You have said—look, I shall put a fleece of wool on the threshing floor; if there is dew on the fleece only, and it is dry on all the ground, then I shall know that You will save Israel by my hand, as You have said." And it was so. When he rose early the next morning and squeezed the fleece together, he wrung the dew out of the fleece, a bowlful of water. Then Gideon said to God, "Do not be angry with me, but let me speak just once more: Let me test, I pray, just once more with the fleece; let it now be dry only on the fleece, but on all the ground let there be dew." And God did so that night. It was dry on the fleece only, but there was dew on all the ground. (Judges 6:36–40)

Though the Lord graciously consented to his request (as He had to a similar one by Moses in Exodus 33:12ff), Gideon's actions should not be viewed as a pattern for believers to follow. As Christians, we do not ascertain the validity of God's Word by asking Him for miraculous confirmation. Instead, we live according to His will by believing Him and being obedient to His Word. The Lord had already told Gideon that He would be victorious over the Midianites. That revelation should have been sufficient. By asking the Lord not to be angry with him before his request, Gideon, driven by his doubt, showed that even he knew he had overstepped his bounds. He acknowledged his faith was weak, but that he was in danger of sinfully putting God to the test (cf. Deuteronomy 6:16).

When his doubts had been removed and he was convinced that the Lord would give him victory, Gideon readied his army of thirty-two thousand men to face the Midianites, likely with a conventional battle strategy. But God had His own strategy for Israel's army—one that could only be disastrous from a human perspective. As they were encamped across the valley from their enemies, the Lord came to Gideon with His shocking plan.

> And the LORD said to Gideon, "The people who are with you are too many for Me to give the Midianites into their hands, lest Israel claim glory for itself against Me, saying, 'My own hand has saved me.' Now therefore, proclaim in the hearing of the people, saying, 'Whoever is fearful and afraid, let him turn and depart at once from Mount Gilead.'" And twenty-two thousand of the people returned, and ten thousand remained. (Judges 7:2–3)

God had chosen timid Gideon to lead the attack so that His glorious power might be the only explanation for victory. Now He instructed the apprehensive leader to downsize the army! If Gideon had been nervous with an army of thirty-two thousand, imagine how he felt when twenty-two thousand of his troops left for home. Gideon would have been helped if he had remembered the words of Moses, who told the Israelites many years earlier, "When you go out to battle against your enemies, and see horses and chariots and people more numerous than you, do not be afraid of them; for the LORD your God is with you" (Deuteronomy 20:1). By reducing the size of the army, God made it certain that this would not be a conventional victory by the men of Israel.

Though only ten thousand warriors were left, God wasn't finished slimming down Israel's forces. In Judges 7:4, He tells Gideon, "The people are still too many." Following the Lord's instructions, Gideon led the army to a nearby brook for a drink. "And the LORD said to Gideon, 'Everyone who laps from the water with his tongue, as a dog laps, you shall set apart by himself; likewise everyone who gets down on his knees to drink'" (v. 5). Of the ten thousand remaining warriors, ninety-seven hundred of them knelt to drink. Only three hundred drank in an unconventional way, lapping the water like a dog. Gideon's faint heart must have nearly stopped when God told him, "By the three hundred men who lapped I will save you, and deliver the Midianites into your hand. Let all the other people go, every man to his place" (v. 7). No reason for such a distinction is given, so the drinking action indicated nothing about their ability as soldiers. It was merely a way to divide the crowd. Their prowess as soldiers had no bearing on the victory.

From the standpoint of proven military tactics, reducing one's army from thirty-two thousand to three hundred makes no sense. But the Lord was declaring an unmistakable point—not just for Gideon but for all of Israel and for us. They were about to see His power put on display; it was time for them to be courageous, not because they themselves were strong, but because the Lord fought on their behalf (cf. Joshua 23:10).

Still, Gideon's fear was palpable (Judges 7:10). So, a third time, God gave him a sign to calm his nerves. It came in a strange way. God instructed Gideon to sneak down to the Midianite camp. He obeyed the frightening demand. When he arrived, he overheard two enemy soldiers conversing. The first reported an odd dream he had experienced the night before, in which a loaf of bread rolled into the Midianite camp and knocked down a tent. In response, the second soldier offered an interpretation, "This is nothing else but the sword of Gideon the son of Joash, a man of Israel! Into his hand God has delivered Midian and the whole camp" (v. 14). After hearing the dream and the terror in his enemy's voice, Gideon had his sign and returned to his troops convinced that the Lord would give them the victory.

THE ARMY THAT ANNIHILATED ITSELF

In the deep darkness of the night, Gideon's three hundred men—having been divided into three companies of one hundred soldiers each—did as they were instructed and took trumpets and torches concealed in empty pitchers and positioned themselves above and around the Midianite camp. In a coordinated effort, Gideon's army blew their trumpets, smashed their pitchers to the ground, held up their blazing torches in the night, and shouted, "The sword of the LORD and of Gideon!" With that cry, the silent stillness of the black night was shattered with blasting trumpets, yelling soldiers, and the sudden blaze of three hundred torches. The strategy was perhaps to make it appear that each of the three hundred represented a whole unit of soldiers.

For Israel's startled enemies, terror followed shock. Dazed and disoriented, the half-asleep Midianites panicked. Thinking there must be Israelite soldiers everywhere in their camp, and in the depth of the darkness, the Midianites were unable to distinguish friend from enemy, and with their swords they slashed a path of escape through their own men. According to Judges 7:21–22, "The whole army ran and cried out and fled. When the three hundred blew the trumpets, the LORD set every man's sword against his companion throughout the whole camp." Thus, the confused Midianite army destroyed itself. Those who managed to escape fled, and Gideon's three hundred gave chase. They also called on other Israelites to help in the pursuit (Judges 7:23).

The rest of Judges 7–8 describes the victorious pursuit of Gideon and his army, as they drove the Midianites out of Israel for good. As a result of the conquest, the Israelites wanted to make him their king, but Gideon acknowledged that the Lord alone was the true King (Judges 8:23). He recognized that all the credit for Israel's deliverance belonged to Almighty God.

Though Gideon did not always make wise choices (cf. Judges 8:24–31), the rest of his lifetime marked an era of peace for the Hebrew nation. In the words of Judges 8:28, "Thus Midian was subdued before the children of Israel, so that they lifted their heads no more. And the country was quiet for forty years in the days of Gideon."

Incredibly, the Lord used this faint-hearted grain farmer to deliver His people from their deadly enemies. When we were first introduced to Gideon, he was sneaking around like a coward, hiding in a winepress. He was the most unlikely of potential heroes. But God elevated him to win a decisive battle against impossible odds—not to exalt Gideon—but to demonstrate His mighty power to save His people. In response, Gideon rightly recognized that the Lord alone deserved all the glory. The young man's dramatic transformation, from faithless to fearless, is such that he is included in the New Testament among the elite examples of the heroes of faith (Hebrews 11:32). His example of faith-filled dependence on the Lord serves as a perpetual reminder of the strength that God supplies to those who trust in Him.

SAMSON: A STRONG MAN MADE WEAK

Gideon's story is enriched when placed alongside the biblical account of another familiar figure. Several generations after Gideon, the Lord raised up a judge in Israel named Samson. The beginnings of their stories share some remarkable parallels. Yet, in terms of their personal dispositions, Gideon and Samson could not have been more opposite. Whereas Gideon was timid and fearful, Samson was brash and reckless. The former saw himself as weak and inadequate; the latter arrogantly believed himself to be invincible. Despite those stark contrasts, the Lord worked through both men to fulfill His sovereign purposes for Israel.

Samson himself is a study in contradiction—a man endowed with supernatural strength whose feats of might belong to the world of children's fantasy heroes. Yet that unparalleled strength and power, corrupted and forfeited by his untamed passion, diminished him into a tragically pitiful weakling. But when he was weakest, the Lord used Samson in the mightiest act of his astonishing life.

BORN TO BE WILD?

In the thirteenth chapter of Judges, Samson's story begins much like Gideon's did. The Israelites were, once again, under the thumb of a foreign enemy: the Philistines. After years of oppression, the Angel of the Lord—another pre-incarnate appearance of the Son of God—came to commission a new deliverer for His people. In this case, He presented Himself to Samson's parents, announcing to them that they would soon have a son who would one day be used by God to rescue the nation. Samson's father, Manoah, responded to the Angel's report in the same way Gideon had—by bringing a young goat and some grain as an offering to the Lord. What happened next is recorded in Judges 13:19–20:

> So Manoah took the young goat with the grain offering, and offered it upon the rock to the LORD. And He did a wondrous thing while Manoah and his wife looked on—it happened as the flame went up toward heaven from the altar—the Angel of the LORD ascended in the flame of the altar! When Manoah and his wife saw this, they fell on their faces to the ground.

As He had done for Gideon, the Lord turned the sacrifice into a miraculous verification of His divine identity. Manoah and his wife were understandably filled with terror when they realized that they had seen God (Judges 13:22). Like Gideon, they thought they were going to die in divine judgment because they were sinners (cf. Judges 6:22–23).

Samson's mother had been barren before the Angel of the Lord promised her that she would give birth to a unique son. The Lord also gave her specific instructions regarding her pregnancy. She was not to drink wine or eat anything that was ceremonially unclean. Also, after the child was born, she was not to cut his hair because Samson was to be a Nazirite. The word *Nazirite* comes from the Hebrew word meaning, "to separate." In Numbers 6:1–8, the Lord gave specific restrictions for those who took this vow of separation: no drinking of alcohol, no cutting of the hair, and no touching of a dead body. This was to externally symbolize the person's commitment to holy living.

The fact that Samson from birth was to be separated had little effect on how he actually lived as an adult. Throughout his life, he would violate all three of the Nazirite prohibitions (touching a dead body—in Judges 14:8–9; drinking at his wedding feast—in Judges 14:10–11; and allowing his head to be shaved—in Judges 16:19). He became a man driven by fleshly desires, especially his illicit and unrestrained passion for pagan women. Scripture describes him as having a stubborn will, irrational desires, and a violent temper— a volatile combination. Ultimately, Samson's wild disregard for the Lord's clear commands would make his life a legendary tragedy, with his infatuation for Philistine women at the center.

Crashing His Own Wedding

In spite of Samson's flagrant sin, for which he paid a terrible price, God still had a purpose for him to serve in rescuing Israel from Philistine aggression. When God wanted him to have supernatural empowerment for his appointed role, the Spirit of the Lord would come upon him and he would display humanly impossible feats of strength, always related to the destruction of the Philistines.

It all was launched when, as a young man, Samson insisted on marrying a Philistine woman—a union that was expressly forbidden by God (Deuteronomy 7:1–5; cf. Judges 3:5–7). The text emphasizes the fact that Samson "saw" the young woman and that she was pleasing *in his sight*, implying that his interest in her was entirely superficial. Though his parents tried to dissuade him from the marriage, Samson ignored their counsel and persisted until he got his way (Judges 14:3).

While walking to the town where his pagan fiancée lived, Samson was ambushed by a lion, an event not unheard of in ancient Israel. Normally, the odds would favor the large predatory cat, with its sharp claws and ferocious fangs. But this time, the lion was to be the victim, as God protected Samson for future exploits. According to Judges 14:6, "The Spirit of the LORD came mightily upon [Samson], and he tore the lion apart as one would have torn apart a young goat, though he had nothing in his hand." Several months later, when Samson passed that way again, he saw the lion's carcass and went to investigate, probably expecting it to be full of flies and maggots. Instead, a colony of bees had taken up residence inside. Avoiding the dead body was required by his Nazirite vow, but Samson ignored that and collected honey from the carcass, eating it as he walked along the road. He even offered some to his parents when he arrived home.

When the betrothal period terminated and wedding preparations were complete, Samson travelled back to his fiancée's hometown for the feast. Such pagan celebrations typically lasted seven days and primarily consisted of drunken revelry. The biblical text indicates that Samson was joined by thirty Philistine young men, whose relationship to him is somewhat unclear. They must have been acquaintances of the bride who had been invited as guests to the feast, and they may also have been guards ordered to watch Samson, whom the Philistines probably already viewed with suspicion. In an effort to embarrass them, the young groom, who was likely drunk himself, challenged the Philistine men with an impossible riddle based on his lion-killing adventure.

> Then Samson said to them, "Let me pose a riddle to you. If you can correctly solve and explain it to me within the seven days of the feast, then I will give you thirty linen garments and thirty changes of clothing. But if you cannot explain it to me, then you shall give me thirty linen garments and thirty changes of clothing." And they said to him, "Pose your riddle, that we may hear it." So he said to them: "Out of the eater came something to eat, And out of the strong came something sweet." Now for three days they could not explain the riddle. (Judges 14:12–14)

Out of frustration over their inability to solve the riddle, the thirty humiliated men cornered Samson's wife, threatening to burn her and her father's house unless she told them the meaning of her husband's riddle. In a preview of Samson's later relationship with Delilah, his bride incessantly begged him to reveal the riddle to her. He initially refused, but her relentless pleading eventually won out.

When the Philistine men produced the correct answer, Samson knew his new bride had betrayed him. Enraged, he traveled to Ashkelon (a Philistine city twenty-three miles away), killed thirty men, and brought back their garments in order to make good on his promised reward for soving the riddle (Judges 14:19). Still fuming, after his slaughter had fed his fury, he left the woman and returned to his parents.

It is sadly ironic that, though identified as one of his nation's foremost judges, Samson never made any attempt to drive Israel's enemies out of the land. In fact, he was happy to interact with the Philistines, even to the point of marrying one of them. Though he was only interested in serving himself, the Lord would superintend Samson's selfish choices to secure Israel's deliverance and ensure Philistia's demise (cf. Judges 14:4).

PLAYING WITH FIRE

Samson's nightmarish wedding likely occurred in early spring-time. After sulking at home for a while, he decided to return to his wife around the time of the wheat harvest. But unknown to Samson, his Philistine father-in-law, who assumed the angry groom would never return, had given his daughter away to someone else (Judges 14:20).

Samson showed up at his wife's house with a young goat, apparently a meager peace offering he hoped would appease the family agitated by the wedding debacle. To his surprise, he was met at the door only by his father-in-law, who refused to let him in. Thoughts of reconciliation turned to rage as Samson heard his father-in-law say the unthinkable: "I really thought that you thoroughly hated her; therefore I gave her to your companion. Is not her younger sister better than she? Please, take her instead" (Judges 15:2).

The betrayed bridegroom was understandably furious, and again he took out his anger on the Philistines. In an incredible feat of superhuman ability, Samson captured three hundred "foxes" and tied their tails together to create one hundred fifty yelping pairs. The Hebrew word for *fox* can also be translated *jackal*. It is likely that jackals were the actual animals involved in this episode since they were more plentiful than foxes in ancient Israel. Having secured the coyote-like creatures together, Samson attached torches to their tails, lit the torches on fire, and sent them frantically zigzagging through the nearby grain fields. With kindled wrath, he used them to ignite the Philistine crops in a blaze that destroyed everything in its path, from grain fields to vineyards to olive groves (Judges 15:5).

When they learned why he had started the fires, the Philistines blamed Samson's former in-laws. They retaliated by burning both his former wife and father-in-law to death (Judges 15:6). Ironically, in order to avoid death earlier, Samson's wife had begged him to reveal the meaning of his riddle to her so she could tell the thirty Philistines at the wedding. Yet by doing that, she set in motion a series of events that ended with the very outcome she had desperately tried to avoid—her own death.

Upon hearing the news of his wife's brutal execution, Samson again became enraged. He accepted no blame for the circumstances leading to her death. Instead, he launched further vengeance against the Philistines. According to Judges 15:8, "he attacked them hip and thigh with a great slaughter; then he went down and dwelt in the cleft of the rock of Etam." The phrase "hip and thigh" can be more accurately translated as "leg upon thigh," and is likely a wrestling idiom for total and violent domination. Here is the providence of God and the fulfillment of divine purpose in a most unimaginable manner. The Lord was using Samson's self-centered rage and revenge to defeat the Philistines.

ESCAPING ARREST

With their fields scorched and their kinsmen slain, the Philistines had enough; they gathered an army and came looking for Samson. The men of Judah saw them approaching and asked, "Why have you come up against us?" The Philistine answer was simple and direct, "We have come up to arrest Samson, to do to him as he has done to us" (Judges 15:10).

Samson's reputation was such that even his fellow Israelites were afraid of him. Accordingly, the men of Judah sent their own army of three thousand men to find him and bring him back to the Philistines. When they located Samson, they asked him, "Do you not know that the Philistines rule over us? What is this you have done to us?" Samson's response, full of self-vindication, was nearly identical to what the Philistines had said just a short time before, "As they did to me, so I have done to them" (Judges 15:11).

An awkward and tense standoff ensued, as the Israelite soldiers announced that they had come to arrest Samson and deliver him to the Philistines. The three thousand men against him posed no threat to Samson. He knew they had been coerced to come after him.

So after making them swear that they would not kill him, Samson agreed to give himself up and go quietly. To prevent his escape, the soldiers bound him with two new ropes.

As the cohort returned to deliver Samson to his enemies, "the Philistines came shouting against him. Then the Spirit of the LORD came mightily upon him; and the ropes that were on his arms became like flax that is burned with fire, and his bonds broke loose from his hands" (Judges 15:14). Snapping away the new ropes, Samson faced his attackers like a real-life superhero. He picked up the nearest object he could find to use as a weapon—the jawbone of a donkey lying on the ground—and ran to confront his enemies.

The Israelite soldiers watched in shock as their former captive single-handedly decimated the army of oppressors. One can hardly imagine the chaos and carnage of that conflict, as Samson slaughtered a thousand of his enemies by himself, with nothing but a nine-inch jawbone. When the battle was over and any surviving Philistines had fled, Samson piled the bodies of his slain adversaries in a heap, and called the place "Ramath Lehi" which means "Jawbone Hill."

Samson, claiming the credit for himself, composed a song to celebrate his victory (Judges 15:16). He was vividly reminded very soon, however, of the fact that God was the source of his strength. Exhausted from the battle, Samson became exceedingly thirsty—to the point of death. He cried out to the Lord in desperation, "You have given this great deliverance by the hand of Your servant; and now shall I die of thirst and fall into the hand of the uncircumcised?" (Judges 15:18).

In spite of Samson's arrogant presumption, he bowed to the reality that "You [God] have given this great deliverance." God responded, answering his prayer by miraculously bringing water from a rock. In the same way that the Lord delivered the grumbling Israelites in the wilderness during the days of Moses (Exodus 17:6), He now delivered Samson from life-threatening dehydration. For the first time in Samson's life, he experienced severe physical weakness and cried out to the Lord for help. He would have to do so again at the end of his life.

After recounting this episode, the biblical text states that Samson "judged Israel twenty years in the days of the Philistines" (Judges 15:20). For two decades, under his protection, the Israelites enjoyed a time of reprieve. Although the Philistines would continue to trouble Israel long after Samson's lifetime, he had broken the back of their dominance. And in his death he struck them with the final, fatal blow.

FATAL ATTRACTION

The closing drama of Samson's life features a man who completely failed to advance from the reckless impulsiveness of his youth. The final chapter began when, as before, he fell for a Philistine woman. But even before he met Delilah, the text notes that he visited a prostitute in Gaza (Judges 16:1–3). While he was with her, the men of Gaza were informed and attempted to capture him. Escaping their effort, Samson uprooted the heavy city gates and carried them (bars and all) on his shoulders to the hills of Hebron, thirty-eight miles away!

The sordid episode in Gaza highlighted both Samson's superhuman strength and his super-sinful weakness. His fatal attraction to pagan women was not only the pattern of his life, but proved to be the path to his death. If Samson were Superman, his own sinful desires were his kryptonite. He could kill a lion, but not his lust. He could break new ropes, but not old habits. He could defeat armies of Philistine soldiers, but not his own flesh. He could carry away the gates of a city but allowed himself to be carried away when lost in passion.

When Samson fixed his lust on Delilah, disaster was inevitable. And the path to that disaster was familiar. Just as Samson's wife had been coerced by the Philistines to learn the answer to her husband's riddle, so Delilah was enticed to discover the secret of Samson's strength. Rather than a threat, as in the first case, this time the Philistine rulers offered Delilah an exorbitant amount of money—fifty-five hundred shekels of silver. Biblical scholars have noted that the average yearly wage for a laborer was only ten silver shekels, making this offer five hundred fifty times that amount! If we compared that to wages of $50,000 today, the cash reward would have been almost $30 million. No amount was too high to eliminate their deadly enemy.

With a fortune at stake, Delilah was happy to seduce her Hebrew boyfriend. She employed the same tactics that Samson's wife had used two decades, and two chapters, earlier—manipulating him by complaining that he did not truly love her (Judges 16:15). Delilah's probing questions were anything but subtle: "Please tell me where your great strength lies, and with what you may be bound to afflict you" (Judges 16:6). And her repeated attempts to trap Samson (in vv. 8, 10, and 14) were a dead giveaway as to the nature of her intentions. Perhaps Samson initially found the game of cat and mouse to be amusing. But eventually Delilah's persistence melted his resolve and he succumbed and told her the truth about his strength.

> And it came to pass, when she pestered him daily with her words and pressed him, so that his soul was vexed to death, that he told her all his heart, and said to her, "No razor has ever come upon my head, for I have been a Nazirite to God from my mother's womb. If I am shaven, then my strength will leave me, and I shall become weak, and be like any other man." (Judges 16:16–17)

Delilah wasted no time. She coaxed Samson to sleep and called for a local barber (v. 19). When the Philistine guards arrived to apprehend him, Samson was helpless. The harrowing words of the text, "he did not know that the LORD had departed from him," express the shock and dismay that Samson suddenly felt. Never before had he been unable to overpower all enemies; never again would he escape from their custody. Still, God Himself would overpower Samson's defeat to bring Israel victory.

BRINGING DOWN THE HOUSE

Samson, so long blinded by might, arrogance, and lust, was now blinded by his captors, who gouged out his eyes and put him to work as a grinder in the prison at Gaza (v. 21). The strongman who had triumphantly carried off the city gates was now utterly humiliated, a prisoner grinding grain with a hand mill in a dungeon. In this, the time of his most desperate weakness, the stage was set for the expression of his greatest strength and the most deadly act of his amazing life.

The Philistines gave the credit for Samson's defeat to their god, Dagon, for whom they held a great celebration in their temple. As the festivities escalated and the madness increased, they demanded to have the defeated strongman come and entertain them (Judges 16:25). Utterly debased, Samson was led into the temple, where he became the butt of coarse jokes and taunts by the crowd as he stumbled blindly to their scornful jests. He asked what seemed like a small courtesy to such a wretched figure—to be led between the central pillars so that he could steady himself by leaning on them.

Archaeological evidence from this time period indicates that Philistine temples had roofs supported by wooden columns planted on short cylindrical foundation stones. The central columns were set close together as the main support for the ceiling. From an engineering perspective, the weight of the perimeter would be drawn to these center pillars and down to the foundation. These columns were so critical that without them the roof would collapse under its own weight.

Samson, without seeing anything, knew he was right where he needed to be. In one final prayer, he asked the Lord to give him back his strength for a climactic, self-sacrificing, heroic act. According to Judges 16:27–28,

> Now the temple was full of men and women. All the lords of the Philistines were there—about three thousand men and women on the roof watching while Samson performed. Then Samson

called to the LORD, saying, "O LORD GOD, remember me, I pray! Strengthen me, I pray, just this once, O God, that I may with one blow take vengeance on the Philistines for my two eyes!"

While personal vengeance was on his mind, and that is not heroic (Romans 12:17–20), Samson had been for many years a judge in Israel, seeking to protect and preserve God's covenant people from the terrorizing Philistines. Beyond his desire for retaliation, the blinded prisoner exhibited a willingness to give his life to protect his people from their deadly enemies. At one time, he had been enamored with Philistine women and they brought him nothing but tragedy. Now he was prepared to kill all of them in that place.

In a miraculous flash of divine energy, supernatural strength poured into his body. The disgraced prisoner offered his last battle cry: "Let me die with the Philistines!" With one hand on each column, Samson began to push, perhaps testing to see if his prayer had been answered. As those immovable monolithic beams began to shift, he knew God had heard and empowered him.

With a surge of incomprehensible power, Samson dislodged the columns so that with a catastrophic crash, the entire wood, stone, and plaster structure collapsed, crushing everyone. The Philistine rulers who had orchestrated his capture were all killed in the destruction, along with three thousand of their celebrating countrymen. Samson had slain hundreds of Philistines during his lifetime, but he had never done anything like this. As Judges 16:30 records, "So the dead that he killed at his death were more than he had killed in his life."

Samson died for the cause of his country and his God. As a divinely appointed deliverer in Israel, he was acting as the Lord's instrument of judgment on His enemies. To be sure, Samson's motives were not entirely pure; his faith was mixed with an unrighteous attitude of personal revenge. Yet as with Rahab and her lie (in Joshua 2:4–5), God honored Samson's faith in spite of his sin.

In terms of brute strength, Samson was the greatest champion in all of Israel's history. Yet he was also a man with horrendous faults. Even so, he is included—along with Gideon—in the list of those who walked by faith (Hebrews 11:32). His final act of valor shows that, in the humiliation and brokenness of his last days, he had come to truly depend on the Lord. He became a hero of faith by trusting God to use him in death and bring him into His presence.

THE WEAKNESS OF MEN AND THE POWER OF GOD

Gideon and Samson represent opposite extremes. Yet both their stories teach the same basic lesson—God's mighty power can override human weakness to accomplish His sovereign purposes. Gideon was a faint-hearted coward who, through the Lord's strength, delivered Israel by conquering the Midianites. Samson was an audacious strongman who, along with his superhuman strength, exhibited super-sinful weakness. Yet the Lord graciously crushed and humbled him so he could be the divine weapon to accomplish victory for the Israelites over the Philistines.

Both these men are presented as examples of faith in the New Testament. Their legacies might best be summarized by the phrase in Hebrews 11:34, "out of weakness [they] were made strong." It was in their moments of greatest frailty, when they were most dependent on the Lord through faith, that they were the strongest because that was when God's power was displayed through them. Their heroism in the redemptive purposes of God was inseparably tied to their humiliation.

So it is with us. As Paul told the Corinthians, the church does not consist of particularly wise, noble, or mighty people (1 Corinthians 1:26). Left to ourselves, we are foolish, base, and weak. But in Christ, we who are inherently worthless and sinful are transformed into vessels of honor, fit for the Master's use. We are thus enabled to serve Him in the strength that He supplies, by His grace and for His glory.

Spiritual victory and usefulness begin with genuine humility, brokenness, and self-distrust—turning to God as the only true power. In the words of the apostle Paul, speaking from the experience of his own suffering and weakness:

> Concerning this [hardship] I pleaded with the Lord three times that it might depart from me. And He said to me, "My grace is sufficient for you, for My strength is made perfect in weakness." Therefore most gladly I will rather boast in my infirmities, that the power of Christ may rest upon me. Therefore I take pleasure in infirmities, in reproaches, in needs, in persecutions, in distresses, for Christ's sake. For when I am weak, then I am strong. (2 Corinthians 12:8–10)

5

JONATHAN: THE MAN WHO
WOULD (NOT) BE KING

———

Then Jonathan, Saul's son, arose and went to David in the woods and strengthened his hand in God. And he said to him, "Do not fear, for the hand of Saul my father shall not find you. You shall be king over Israel, and I shall be next to you."

—1 SAMUEL 23:16–17

T HE LAST OF THE OLD TESTAMENT judges looked in disbelief at the group of Israelite leaders assembled before him. For his entire life, Samuel had led the nation with integrity and wisdom as God's appointed judge and prophet. But he was now an old man, no other judges were on the horizon, and his sons were morally unfit to take his place (1 Samuel 8:3). Nonetheless, it was still shocking and hurtful for him to hear what the elders of the people had come to say.

As they gathered in the village of Ramah, Samuel's hometown, the Israelites wasted no time letting the distinguished prophet-judge know that they were actively looking for his replacement, even before he was dead. And it wouldn't be another judge or prophet, if they had their way. Their words undoubtedly cut Samuel to the core: "Look, you are old, and your sons do not walk in your ways. Now make us a king to judge us like all the nations" (1 Samuel 8:5). With that one request, the period of the judges came to a screeching halt after three hundred fifty years. A divinely appointed judge and prophet was not enough to satisfy the people; they wanted to be like the surrounding nations—they wanted a king.

Understandably, Samuel felt the pain of being slighted by the Israelites' impetuous request; he interpreted their words as a personal attack on him and his ministry. But the Lord informed him that a far greater offense was actually taking place. "Heed the voice of the people in all that they say to you," the Lord told Samuel. "For they have not rejected you, but they have rejected Me, that I should not reign over them" (1 Samuel 8:7).

Ever since the Israelites promised at Mount Sinai to serve and obey God (Exodus 19:5–8), the nation had functioned as a *theocracy*. The Lord was the only King in Israel, and He governed through the complex of judges, prophets, and priests whom he appointed to represent Him among His people. When the Israelites asked Samuel for a human king, they were simply articulating their discontent with the rule of God. They no longer wanted the theocracy—but rather a *monarchy* like their foreign neighbors. Throughout the previous four centuries, they had repeatedly forsaken the Lord to worship other gods. Their request for a human king was the final expression of that recycling apostasy so often demonstrated in rebellion against their true Sovereign (1 Samuel 8:8).

Samuel warned the people about the inevitable downside of having a monarch. Kings forced their populace to labor in their fields and to fashion their military equipment; they drafted sons into their armies and took daughters captive to work as perfumers, cooks, and bakers in their royal service. For their own purposes, kings seized land, forced payment of taxes and tribute, took possessions at will, and made subjects, servants, and slaves of the populace. In all these ways, the people would forfeit their freedom and even be abused. Samuel's final words of warning were the most frightening of all: "And you will cry out in that day because of your king whom you have chosen for yourselves, and the LORD will not hear you in that day" (1 Samuel 8:18). Once they set up earthly kings in power to replace the true King, there would be no turning back. The monarchy would bring disaster and even divine judgment.

Still the Israelites stubbornly insisted. Refusing to heed Samuel's warning, they impudently responded, "No, but we will have a king over us, that we also may be like all the nations, and that our king may judge us and go out before us and fight our battles" (vv. 19–20). During the reign of Israel's first king, Saul, the worst possible outcomes would begin to manifest themselves, just as Samuel had warned.

ISRAEL'S FIRST ROYAL FAMILY

Our story is about a son of Saul named Jonathan, to whom we are introduced in 1 Samuel 13:2. He did not grow up in the house of a king, but rather in the home of a farmer. When he was a teenager, several of his grandfather's donkeys went missing, and Jonathan's father, Saul, went looking for them (1 Samuel 9:3). An extensive search failed to locate the missing animals; instead, Saul ran into the prophet Samuel. "As for your donkeys that were lost three days ago, do not be anxious about them, for they have been found," Samuel assured the forlorn farmer (v. 20). But it was what the prophet said next that Saul could never have expected, "And on whom is all the desire of Israel? Is it not on you and on all your father's house?" To Saul's shock, Samuel explained that he would become Israel's first king. What had started at the low level as a hunt for missing donkeys ended at unexpected heights, with the startling promise that the donkey-hunter would become king!

Tall, handsome, and from the warrior-tribe of Benjamin, Saul was the ideal candidate for Israel's first monarch—judging by external appearances. In reality, his physical attributes merely hid a tragic weakness of character that was below the surface to start with, but would be unmistakably revealed during his long tenure as king. According to Acts 13:21, Saul reigned over Israel for forty years, but his shortcomings surfaced almost immediately. When he returned home from meeting with Samuel, Saul shyly kept his coming position a secret (1 Samuel 10:16); and later, during his public coronation ceremony, he tried to hide (v. 22). Timid insecurity continually characterized his rule. Fear and faltering confidence evidenced itself repeatedly throughout his reign as he grew paranoid of potential rivals and acted rashly to compensate for his ineptness as a leader.

One wonders how Saul's family and especially his oldest son, Jonathan, responded when they first heard the astonishing news. Jonathan's brain was undoubtedly sifting through all kinds of expectations and probabilities as he considered his father's newfound responsibilities—along with his own role as the prince. Did this mean that he would one day be king himself? Aware of his father's weaknesses, and familiar with his former role as a farmer, Jonathan was not intimidated by Saul's unexpected promotion. In fact, he did not hesitate to defy his father's authority when Israel's new monarch acted in utterly irrational ways.

JONATHAN AND SAUL: LIKE FATHER LIKE SON?

Israel's primary expectation for its new king was that he would protect and deliver them from their enemies (1 Samuel 8:20). Almost immediately, the legitimacy of that anticipation was successfully put to the test, as Saul led the Israelites to a God-given victory over the Ammonites (1 Samuel 11:13). A greater challenge came less than two years into Saul's reign, when accompanied by a standing army of three thousand men, the king found himself in a dangerous conflict with the Philistines. Though Samson had earlier dealt a devastating blow to the Philistines, they still presented a military threat to Israel in Saul's day. Israel's new monarch had no need to fear, however, because the Lord had already promised to deliver them into his hand (1 Samuel 9:16).

It is in the context of this conflict that Jonathan first appears in the biblical record. He was likely in his late teens or early twenties—old enough to be placed in charge of one thousand of his father's forces (1 Samuel 13:2). While Saul waited elsewhere, Jonathan with his men attacked the Philistine garrison in Geba and captured it. Geba was located about three miles from Israel's original capitol, the city of Gibeah, making the destruction of this Philistine outpost of great strategic importance to the new monarchy. Whether Saul ordered the attack is not stated. In either case, it was Jonathan, not Saul, who initiated this critical military action. The conflict quickly escalated into full-scale war, giving opportunity for Jonathan to prove himself a more courageous and capable leader than his apprehensive father.

Saul's Foolish Disobedience

The Israelites may have expected a relatively small, measured retaliation from their enemies, but instead, their aggression was met with the full fury and force of the Philistine military. Thousands of chariots, horsemen, and infantry—"as the sand which is on the seashore in multitude" (1 Samuel 13:5)—assembled to rain vengeance on the Hebrew army, which appeared puny in comparison. Saul's men reacted not in faith and courage, but in total fear. Many of his soldiers abandoned him, hiding "in caves, in thickets, in rocks, in holes, and in pits" (v. 6), or crossing the Jordan River and leaving the land altogether. So many fled that his initial fighting force dwindled to only six hundred fighters (v.15)! So he waited in mortal fear in Gilgal.

Saul actually had no reason to be paralyzed by the fear of massacre and death because Samuel had earlier given him clear instructions about how to respond at Gilgal:

"You shall go down before me to Gilgal; and surely I will come down to you to offer burnt offerings and make sacrifices of peace offerings. Seven days you shall wait, till I come to you and show you what you should do." (1 Samuel 10:8)

That week must have felt like an eternity, both for Saul and for those who stayed with him. In their minds, Samuel could not come quickly enough! Their hearts were filled with dread, as scouts reported daily of the growing Philistine host threatening to destroy them.

On the seventh day, when it seemed as though Samuel was not coming to offer the sacrifices, Saul's faith collapsed. In desperation, he determined that he could wait no longer; his enemy was only getting stronger and bolder while his own forces were dissipating in cowardice. Feeling compelled to take some action, in disregard for Samuel's instructions, Saul decided to offer the sacrifices himself (1 Samuel 13:9). Sadly, this would not be the last time in Saul's royal career that he tried to obtain the Lord's blessing through an act of disobedience.

Like a scene from a classic comedy sketch, as soon as Saul offered the sacrifices, Samuel showed up. But the indignant prophet wasn't amused. The king went out eagerly to meet him, woefully unaware just how egregious his invasion into the restricted priestly office had been. Usurping the role of a priest, as Saul had done, had been strictly forbidden in Numbers 3:10 and 18:7. A later king of Judah named Uzziah would similarly learn the hard way that God took such an offense very seriously (2 Chronicles 26:16–21).

Saul was soon to be severely condemned. Samuel's biting question, "What have you done?" rocked Saul's conscience. Like God's question to Adam in Genesis 3:9, Samuel's words to Saul were a stinging indictment for which there was no adequate answer, no valid excuse, and no defense.

But that didn't stop Saul from trying to explain away his sin. When faced with the just accusation of his guilt, Adam had tried to shift the blame. Saul employed that same time-honored "blame-shifting" strategy, with equally disastrous results. He pinned the culpability on everyone but himself—on Samuel for his late arrival, on his troops for their cowardice, and on the Philistines for the ominous threat they represented (1 Samuel 13:11–12). But his blame-shifting only intensified his sin.

Samuel's devastating reply to Saul's attempted evasion made it painfully clear that God held him solely responsible. The stern-faced prophet spoke for God when he told Saul:

> You have done foolishly. You have not kept the commandment of the LORD your God, which He commanded you. For now the LORD would have established your kingdom over Israel forever. But now your kingdom shall not continue. The LORD has sought for Himself a man after His own heart, and the LORD has commanded him to be commander over His people, because you have not kept what the LORD commanded you. (1 Samuel 13:13–14)

Earlier, Samuel had warned the Israelites that—even under their new monarchy—if they failed to obey the Lord, they would be swept away in judgment along with their king (1 Samuel 12:25). Driven by doubt and fear, Saul experienced those severe consequences firsthand. The Lord would choose a replacement for him—someone who, unlike Saul, could be characterized as a "man after [God's] own heart."

Evidently, Jonathan was not in Gilgal when Saul dishonored the Lord and doomed his own dynasty. But the prince would soon learn that God's judgment was not just on Saul but on his family, so that Jonathan would never become king. For most in that position, that realization would kill long-fed expectations and be devastatingly disappointing. Yet as we will see, Jonathan's response was very different—and that's what made him such an unlikely hero.

JONATHAN'S COURAGEOUS FAITH

By foolishly offering sacrifices to the Lord, Saul had violated the sanctity and uniqueness of the priestly office. He also failed to trust the word of God through Samuel. And the consequences were severe. Saul's faithlessness, however, was in bold contrast to the faith of his son, Jonathan. With the Philistine army still encamped nearby, waiting to attack, the young prince took his armor bearer on a dangerous covert mission (1 Samuel 14:1).

The plan was an extremely risky, even irrational, one: free-climb up the face of a craggy cliff and surprise-attack a Philistine garrison accompanied by no one but the armor bearer. First Samuel 14:4 describes the treacherous topography of their intended route: "Between the passes, by which Jonathan sought to go over to the Philistines' garrison, there was a sharp rock on one side and a sharp rock on the other side. And the name of one was Bozez, and the name of the other Seneh." The name *Bozez*, in Hebrew, likely means *slippery*; and the name *Seneh* means *thorny*. Slick rocks and sharp thistles characterized these cliffs! But that was not the worst of it. The perilous path ended at the gates of an enemy outpost. It was a suicide mission.

But listen to Jonathan's unwavering faith. Speaking to his armor bearer, he said, "Come, let us go over to the garrison of these uncircumcised; it may be that the LORD will work for us. For nothing restrains the LORD from saving by many or by few" (v. 6). Jonathan was fearless—not because he was confident in his own ability, but because he had placed his faith firmly in the promised will and power of God. If the Lord fought for them, the two of them would be enough.

That the Lord was going to honor Jonathan's faith was apparent in their first move. After scaling the cliff, he and his armor bearer slew twenty enemy soldiers (vv. 13–14). The ancient Jewish historian Josephus suggests that this attack took place early in the morning and that the element of surprise was increased by the fact that many of the Philistines were still asleep. But whatever the time of day, the reality is that the Lord gave Jonathan and his armor bearer power over twenty soldiers. When the Philistine army heard what had happened, as fleeing soldiers from the garrison brought back reports of the slaughter, they were struck with fear and, despite their overwhelming numbers, began to scatter. The Lord struck further terror in their hearts by causing an earthquake (v. 15) and sending the Philistine soldiers into a confused panic so that they began to kill one another (v. 20). By the time Saul and his army launched the main attack, the battle was all but over.

The Lord responded to the faith and courage of Jonathan by sending the enemy into full retreat, thereby delivering the out-matched Israelites from death and defeat. Jonathan's theology had motivated his battlefield heroics—the Lord was able to deliver with many or with few. Confident in God's power, Jonathan put faith into action. While Saul sat under a pomegranate tree fretting about what to do next, his daring son once again took the initiative and saw the mighty power of God unleashed in victory.

SAUL'S SILLY CURSE

Back before the battle began, Saul's troops had been abandoning him in droves. Their defection, in part, had motivated Saul to disobey God by offering sacrifices before Samuel arrived. It may also explain the petty curse that the desperate king placed on his own men. In an apparent attempt to keep his remaining forces from desertion, Saul overreacted and placed them under a deadly oath: "Cursed is the man who eats any food until evening, before I have taken vengeance on my enemies" (1 Samuel 14:24). His soldiers were thus bound to win the victory before they could even eat their next meal!

Saul's intentions may have been noble, and his oath may have been intended to spark a religiously motivated fast, in which his troops would be so focused on the battle that they wouldn't even think of eating; but whatever his rationale, Saul's plan seriously backfired. His famished troops quickly grew weary in combat, becoming less and less effective in the pursuit of their enemies. More significantly, the soldiers became so hungry that, when finally triumphant and allowed to eat, they gorged themselves and violated God's law by eating meat that was mixed with blood (cf. Leviticus 17:10–14). The king's small-minded oath not only hurt his war effort, but it also caused his people to transgress the law of God.

When Saul subsequently sought divine guidance through the priest, the Lord refused to answer him. (God also chose not to respond to future presumptuous requests made by sinful Saul— 1 Samuel 28:6.) Though he had caused his army to sin badly, Saul took no responsibility for his part in their actions. Predictably, he looked for someone else to blame, and so missed the reason for the Lord's silence. Rather than examining his own actions and repenting, he wrongly assumed God's response was due to someone else's sin. One of his soldiers must have violated the ban on eating! He may have thought that was why the Lord refused to answer him. Hypocritical Saul was determined to discover and punish the culprit, even if it was his own son!

Jonathan and his armor bearer had already left on their covert mission when Saul charged his troops with his unreasonable oath, so the prince was unaware of his father's foolishness. Later that day, however, when the Israelites were chasing fleeing Philistines through a wooded area, Jonathan found honey on the ground, stopped, and ate some. Only in that moment, when Jonathan unwittingly violated his father's curse, did his fellow soldiers inform him of it. Jonathan's response underscored the severity of Saul's actions:

> My father has troubled the land. Look now, how my countenance has brightened because I tasted a little of this honey. How much

better if the people had eaten freely today of the spoil of their enemies which they found! For now would there not have been a
much greater slaughter among the Philistines? (1 Samuel 14:29–30)

When Saul learned that Jonathan had violated his ridiculous
oath, he determined to maintain his puny pride by putting him to
death. After all, everyone knew the king had rashly vowed to kill
the guilty party, no matter who it might be. In shocked protest, the
prince highlighted the absurdity of the situation, "I only tasted a
little honey with the end of the rod that was in my hand. So now
I must die!" (v. 43). But Saul was dead serious. In the face of this
idiocy, the people began interceding on Jonathan's behalf. If not for
them, the king would have executed his firstborn son.

All of this took place during Saul's first major skirmish with
the Philistines, an event that highlighted the extreme differences
between Saul and Jonathan. They were poles apart in nature. The
king was fearful, indecisive, reactionary, disobedient, reckless, proud,
and heavy-handed. Jonathan was exactly the opposite. He took initiative, showed courage, acted humbly and purposefully, exposed his
father's foolishness, and exhibited trusting confidence in the Lord.
By God's power, Jonathan (not Saul) was the one who set in motion
Israel's victory. As Saul's reign continued, and his weaknesses became
increasingly obvious, the contrast between father and son grew only
more pronounced—and that contrast became crystallized into clarity
when a young shepherd named David entered the picture.

JONATHAN AND DAVID: THE
LOVELY VIRTUE OF LOYALTY

By failing to trust the Lord, and by offering sacrifices before Samuel
arrived, Saul proved to be an incompetent leader who left behind
him a royal mess. He only accelerated his self-destruction as his

reign continued. When God commanded him to completely destroy the Amalekites, including all their livestock, Saul again disobeyed. He left the captured King Agag alive and allowed Israel's troops to take the best of the sheep and oxen. As before, the foolish monarch rebelled against the word of the Lord. And once more the consequences were predictably severe.

When Samuel arrived, Saul claimed to have complied with the Lord's instructions. In disbelief, the prophet protested with another penetrating question, "What then is this bleating of the sheep in my ears, and the lowing of the oxen which I hear?" (1 Samuel 15:14). Once again, there was no excuse for Saul's failure to obey. True to form, he blamed his actions on the people and added a noble-sounding footnote: that he intended to use the captured livestock for sacrifices to the Lord.

Samuel's profound and memorable words in response must have hit Saul like a sledgehammer:

> Has the Lord as great delight in burnt offerings and sacrifices,
> As in obeying the voice of the Lord?
> Behold, to obey is better than sacrifice,
> And to heed than the fat of rams.
> For rebellion is as the sin of witchcraft,
> And stubbornness is as iniquity and idolatry.
> Because you have rejected the word of the Lord,
> He also has rejected you from being king. (1 Samuel 15:22–23)

The aged prophet then did what Saul would never have the courage to do; in the presence of all who were watching, as a public rebuke to Saul's compromising failure, the old man picked up a heavy sword and hacked the Amalekite king to pieces (v. 33)! Splattered with blood and flesh, Samuel showed Israel's rebellious king what complete obedience looked like. That vivid drama was Saul's last sight of faithful Samuel before the prophet died.

The prophet-judge had spoken God's truth when he warned

Israel that wanting a king would lead to disaster. And it did. While the disheartened prophet was still grieving over the tragedy of Saul, God instructed him to anoint a replacement from another family to be king in Israel. Unlike Saul, who was physically impressive, the Lord chose an unimpressive shepherd boy. As a pre-teen youth, the youngest of eight brothers, David wasn't the tallest or strongest. But as the Lord reminded Samuel, "The LORD does not see as man sees; for man looks at the outward appearance, but the LORD looks at the heart" (1 Samuel 16:7).

Thus when Saul was still alive and on his tarnished throne, David's royal training began. When an evil spirit terrorized the king, David—already known as a gifted musician—was selected to play the harp for him (vv. 14–23). Still living in Bethlehem, David went to the palace and was given an invaluable introduction to the royal court. When the Philistine giant Goliath threatened the Israelites, the Lord used this young shepherd to kill him with a slingshot, cut off his head, and secure the victory (1 Samuel 17:50). Like Jonathan, David knew that the Lord could save Israel using either many or only a few. No doubt, Jonathan was there when David defeated the colossus under God's power and must have recognized the kindred spirit of one whose faith was in the Lord in the face of deadly enemies.

Sparked by the incident with Goliath, a deep friendship developed between Jonathan and David. First Samuel 18:1 describes the loyalty and devotion that characterized their unusual friendship: "The soul of Jonathan was knit to the soul of David, and Jonathan loved him as his own soul." The name *Jonathan* means "gift from the Lord," and the prince would certainly prove himself to be that for David.

After David's remarkable victory, Saul insisted that this young musician and giant killer come live at the palace. He gave David his own daughter to marry, along with a position of leadership in his army, in addition to his duties as a musician in the royal court. In these and many other ways, the Lord prospered David so that he became immensely popular with the people. Saul—ever fearful and threatened, as well as aware that his dynasty was cursed and his kingdom would not last—soon grew suspicious of the young champion, saw him as his rival, and sought to murder him.

Under this deadly threat, David would have had no chance. But he had an ally in the royal court, his friend and brother-in-law, Jonathan. Their hearts had been knit together such that they made a covenant of loyalty to one another (1 Samuel 18:3). When Saul threatened to kill David, the prince warned him of the king's intention. Jonathan even interceded with his father on David's behalf, but that effort left Saul unmoved in his murderous resolve.

David was shocked to learn that Saul wanted him dead. He realized the potential danger; but he wanted to be sure of the king's evil intentions. He devised a simple test to remove any doubts.

> David said to Jonathan, "Indeed tomorrow is the New Moon, and I should not fail to sit with the king to eat. But let me go, that I may hide in the field until the third day at evening. If your father misses me at all, then say, 'David earnestly asked permission of me that he might run over to Bethlehem, his city, for there is a yearly sacrifice there for all the family.' If he says thus: 'It is well,' your servant will be safe. But if he is very angry, be sure that evil is determined by him. (1 Samuel 20:5–7).

Jonathan agreed, and the plan was set in motion.

On the second day after the new moon, when David did not come to the king's table to eat, Saul asked where he was. When Jonathan answered that he had given David permission to be absent, the king became furious—accusing his son of favoring David to his own shame and the shame of his family. In the heat of the moment,

> Saul's anger was aroused against Jonathan, and he said to him, "You son of a perverse, rebellious woman! Do I not know that

you have chosen the son of Jesse to your own shame and to the shame of your mother's nakedness? For as long as the son of Jesse lives on the earth, you shall not be established, nor your kingdom. Now therefore, send and bring him to me, for he shall surely die." (1 Samuel 20:30–31)

When the prince responded by defending his friend's honor, Saul grabbed his spear and, in an uncontrollable fit of rage, launched it across the dinner table at his son's head, narrowly missing his target. Nobody moved. The only sound in the room came from the still-vibrating spear handle plunged ominously into the wall. Silently seething at his father's violent rage, Jonathan made a fast exit.

The next day, the melancholy prince found his way to the field where he and his friend had agreed to convene and discuss the test. As they had prearranged, Jonathan shot an arrow past his servant, and asked him, "Is not the arrow beyond you?" (v. 37). That coded question meant Saul was angry and set to kill David. When the prince's servant had returned to the city, David emerged from his hiding spot to say goodbye to Jonathan, who had remained. The two men wept because David was now a fugitive on the run for his life. Jonathan's parting words to David underscored their loyalty to one another: "Go in peace, since we have both sworn in the name of the LORD, saying, 'May the LORD be between you and me, and between your descendants and my descendants, forever'" (v. 42). David then went into hiding, and Jonathan went back into the city.

Saul spent the rest of his life hunting David. Why this irrational passion? Because he knew the Lord had chosen David to be Israel's next king. David spent those same years as the hunted—fleeing, hiding, and patiently surviving until Saul died. Though Saul nearly captured him on several occasions, the Lord protected David, all the while using the exigencies of his harsh experience to shape him into an exceptional leader and commander.

During those years, on occasion, Jonathan found ways to meet his friend in order to encourage him and reiterate his loyalty to him. Jonathan consistently affirmed what Saul was desperately trying to prevent—that David would be Israel's next king. With remarkable love and humility, the prince explained to David, "Do not fear, for the hand of Saul my father shall not find you. You shall be king over Israel, and I shall be next to you. Even my father Saul knows that" (1 Samuel 23:17).

Jonathan willingly gave up his own claim to the throne because he understood that the Lord had chosen David instead of him. And he had no resentment, only affection for the one who would reign in his place. Ironically, while Saul tenaciously (and futilely) tried to retain the throne for his son, his son happily offered it to the man he knew was God's choice to be Israel's ruler.

Jonathan's character is evidenced most clearly in his attitude toward David. Without question, he was a mighty warrior, a noble prince, and a loyal friend. But it was his unwavering faith in the Lord's plan for him and his future that set him apart as an unlikely hero. Jonathan did not merely *accept* his non-kingly role; he *embraced* it wholeheartedly—eagerly protecting and promoting the one whom God had appointed to be king instead of him.

DAVID AND MEPHIBOSHETH: THE LASTING LEGACY OF KINDNESS

That interaction between David and Jonathan is the last we hear of the prince until a catastrophic battle with the Philistines in which Saul, Jonathan, and two of his brothers were killed (1 Samuel 31:2). The slaughter brought profound grief to David, launching a sorrowful lament recorded in the first chapter of 2 Samuel. From his heart came words of sadness not only for Jonathan, but also for Saul. But David reserved the following loving tribute for his dearly departed friend:

How the mighty have fallen in the midst of the battle!
Jonathan was slain in your high places.
I am distressed for you, my brother Jonathan;
You have been very pleasant to me;
Your love to me was wonderful,
Surpassing the love of women.
How the mighty have fallen,
And the weapons of war perished! (2 Samuel 1:25–27)

In the melancholy of his affection, David emphasized the unusual loyalty that he had shared with the prince. In saying that their friendship surpassed "the love of women," David was not demeaning the bond of love that exists between a husband and wife; rather, he was emphasizing the fact that his love for Jonathan was a love without any physical attraction or interest. That made it altogether unlike the affection shared between a man and a woman, which includes both physical attraction and relations. David and Jonathan shared a manly commitment that was noble, loyal, and selfless—a camaraderie born out of threat and conflict and cemented by their mutual faith in the Lord.

But David's devotion to the well-being of his friend did not cease even after Jonathan died. Years before, he had sworn that his favor would extend to Jonathan's descendants. This pledge by David came in response to his friend's request. Jonathan—certain that David would one day be king—sought to make with him a covenant of protection for his descendants. Knowing the depth of David's love for him, he declared what he knew David was willing to do after his death:

> You shall not only show me the kindness of the LORD while I still live, that I may not die; but you shall not cut off your kindness from my house forever, no, not when the LORD has cut off every one of the enemies of David from the face of the earth." So

Jonathan made a covenant with the house of David, saying, "Let the LORD require it at the hand of David's enemies. (1 Samuel 20:14–16)

David, true to his promise, continued to honor that covenant with his friend.

The most wonderful example of David's covenant loyalty was his response to Jonathan's only son, Mephibosheth. He was only five when his father was killed. His nanny, hearing the horrible news, was afraid that those who killed Saul and his sons would come after the child to take his life, so she picked him up to flee, but in her frightened mad dash, she dropped the young boy and his legs were broken (2 Samuel 4:4). Mephibosheth was permanently crippled as a result of the accident.

Years later, David sought out Mephibosheth—as Jonathan's sole descendant—and invited him to the palace where he was welcomed like one of his own sons, regularly dining at the royal table. David further gave Mephibosheth the land that had previously belonged to his grandfather, Saul, and instructed Saul's former servants to continue working the land for their master's grandson (2 Samuel 9:1–13).

David's kindness toward Mephibosheth was motivated by nothing more than gracious love and covenant faithfulness; as such, his actions give us a wonderful analogy of God's unmerited love for sinners. David took all the initiative. He sought out Mephibosheth and welcomed him to the palace. He did so even though Mephibosheth was the grandson of Saul—Israel's cursed king and David's greatest persecutor. Mephibosheth could do nothing to repay David or offer him any significant service. Nevertheless, David brought him into his family, invited him to his table, and even granted him an inheritance of land to which he was not legally entitled. In grateful response, Mephibosheth became a lifelong, loyal servant to David (cf. 2 Samuel 19:24–30).

Though the lives of most of Saul's descendants were taken, David was careful to protect Mephibosheth "because of the LORD's oath that was between them, between David and Jonathan the son of Saul" (2 Samuel 21:7). Mephibosheth's son, Micah, would sustain the lineage of Jonathan's house—so that his heirs persisted for many generations and produced noble warriors (1 Chronicles 8:34–40). As the prince, Jonathan had been faithful to protect David. Now, as the king, David was faithful to honor his covenant promises to Jonathan by graciously embracing Mephibosheth as a member of his own family.

JONATHAN'S LEGACY

Jonathan, the first prince of Israel, functioned as both a foil to his father and a friend to his father's successor. When Saul should have been initiating the attack on the Philistines, it was Jonathan who led the charge. When Saul was doubtful and disobedient, Jonathan operated in faith and courage. His level-headed response to his father's violent mood swings and irrational behavior set him apart as a striking contrast to the reckless king.

Early into Saul's reign, Jonathan learned that his father's kingdom would never belong to him. A typical response to that kind of disappointment would include anger and resentment. But Jonathan's response was far from typical—which is what makes him such an *unlikely* hero. Rather than fighting against his future, the prince embraced it—to the extent that he became a loyal friend to the man who would one day be king instead of him. While his father tried to destroy David, Jonathan valiantly protected David and defended his reputation—demonstrating heroic loyalty to him at every turn. Though Saul's legacy is one of disobedience, distrust, and disappointment, the legacy of his son Jonathan is completely the opposite. Here was a man who had every reason in the world to be threatened by David, just like his father was. Yet this unlikely hero let his crown go with no remorse and lived for the well-being of the one who would be king in his place, as God had determined.

Jonathan's first-recorded words evidenced his resolute faith in the Lord's will and power—when he told his armor bearer:

> Come, let us go over to the Philistines' garrison that is on the other side. . . . Come, let us go over to the garrison of these uncircumcised; it may be that the LORD will work for us. For nothing restrains the LORD from saving by many or by few. (1 Samuel 14:1, 6)

His last-recorded words, spoken to David, underscore his confidence in God's perfect plan for his future and for Israel:

> Do not fear, for the hand of Saul my father shall not find you. You shall be king over Israel, and I shall be next to you. Even my father Saul knows that. (1 Samuel 23:17)

Unlike his small-minded father, this noble prince was eager to obey the Lord.

So out of the tragic saga of Saul comes the story of Jonathan's heroic selflessness and unwavering friendship. Jesus said, "Greater love has no one than this, than to lay down one's life for his friends" (John 15:13). Without question, Jonathan would have sacrificed his life in death to protect his friend. That is the ultimate sacrifice. But close to it is the sacrifice of one's life *in life*—gladly giving up all personal honor, power, and position for a friend who takes those things because it was the will of God to do so.

6

JONAH: THE WORLD'S
GREATEST FISH STORY

Now the word of the LORD *came to Jonah the second time, saying,*
"Arise, go to Nineveh, that great city, and preach to it the message that
I tell you." So Jonah arose and went to Nineveh, according to the word
of the LORD.

—JONAH 3:1–3A

T HE EXISTENCE OF "ROGUE WAVES" was not scientifically veri-
fied until January 1, 1995, when an eighty-four-foot wall of
water suddenly slammed into the Draupner oil platform off
the coast of Norway. It was more than twice the size of any other
wave recorded that day—an unexpected anomaly of cataclysmic
proportions.

Though only recently validated by science, eyewitness accounts
of such terrifying phenomena, related by surviving sailors, have been
passed down for centuries. Maritime folklore is filled with tales of
these "freak waves," turbulent towers of salt water with troughs so
deep and crests so high that ships might be literally swallowed by the
ocean. Even modern seafaring vessels are susceptible to the power

of such unpredictable and unpreventable forces of nature. In 2001, two cruise ships—the MS *Bremen* and *Caledonian Star*—were both severely damaged by a single ninety-eight-foot rogue wave in the South Atlantic. Other similar incidents have been reported in the years since.

Though infrequent, rogue waves demonstrate just how volatile and precarious the sea can become in extreme conditions. In the midst of a storm, ocean waves commonly reach heights over twenty feet and, in severe conditions, over forty feet. On rare occasions, they can rise to even greater heights. Buoys off the coast of Nova Scotia, during the infamous Halloween Storm of 1991 (known more commonly as "The Perfect Storm"), measured waves in the Atlantic of over a hundred feet. Whipped up by the intense winds of hurricanes and tropical storms, such massive waves are both terrifying and deadly.

The opening chapter of Jonah is set in the midst of that kind of intense storm. Modern meteorology has documented the development of tropical cyclones in the Mediterranean Sea—violent tempests that can produce winds in excess of ninety miles per hour that create surging waves as a result. But the storm recorded in Jonah was qualitatively different from anything that might occur naturally. Jonah 1:4 explains that "the LORD sent out a great wind on the sea," indicating that its cause was *super*natural. The seasoned sailors with whom Jonah traveled—men who had traversed the waters of the Mediterranean their entire lives—had never encountered anything like it before. Undoubtedly, they had survived to tell tales of countless storms in their many voyages, but perhaps none was like this one. The biting wind seemed angry and vengeful as it slammed the helpless ship into massive barricades of oncoming surf. The wooden planks that formed the hull began to splinter and pull apart under the overwhelming pressure. Wave after wave crashed down upon her decks—each resembling a rogue wave in its unrelenting fury and unexplainable magnitude. The white-knuckled crew, clinging on and fearing they would not survive, cried out in panicked desperation. This storm felt personal. Indeed, it was.

A ROGUE PROPHET

While the Gentile sailors frantically scurried about, bailing water and tossing any unnecessary cargo overboard, a seemingly oblivious Hebrew prophet was sound asleep in the hold of the ship. The boat may have been tossing and turning, but, incredibly, Jonah was not. It was only the ship's captain waking him that brought Jonah to conscious awareness of the chaos and deadly danger of the storm.

Once awake, however, Jonah was quickly in the middle of the greatest danger. When the crew cast lots to find who was to blame for angering the gods, Jonah was singled out and his suspicions were confirmed—he was God's target in the tempest. This storm, in fact, had been sent by the Lord both to chastise him for his flagrant disobedience and to halt him from running farther away. With bewildered and anxious faces, the pagan sailors looked to Jonah for an explanation.

> They said to him, "Please tell us! For whose cause is this trouble upon us? What is your occupation? And where do you come from? What is your country? And of what people are you?" So he said to them, "I am a Hebrew; and I fear the Lord, the God of heaven, who made the sea and the dry land." Then the men were exceedingly afraid, and said to him, "Why have you done this?" For the men knew that he fled from the presence of the Lord, because he had told them. (Jonah 1:8–10)

A short time earlier, perhaps only a few weeks or even days, the Lord had come to Jonah with a simple command, "Arise, go to Nineveh, that great city, and cry out against it; for their wickedness has come up before Me" (Jonah 1:2). The mandate was clear and direct: preach a message of repentance or judgment to the Assyrians in their capital city of Nineveh. For Jonah, however, submitting to that directive proved to be inordinately difficult. Instead of heading east toward Assyria, the reluctant prophet fled in the opposite direction. He boarded a ship bound for Tarshish—the westernmost port on the Mediterranean Sea, near modern-day Gibraltar in Spain. But he would soon learn in an astounding way that it is dangerous to try to outrun God (cf. Psalm 139:7–12).

Jonah had his reasons for fleeing in the direction away from Nineveh. The Assyrian capital was situated along the Tigris River (in modern-day Iraq) and boasted a population of six hundred thousand—making it an exceptionally large metropolis for that time. The city was originally built by Nimrod, the great-grandson of Noah, who was likely in charge of the building of the Tower of Babel (Genesis 10:8–11, 11:1–9). It had become the capital city of a pagan enemy nation and represented everything evil that the Israelites hated.

Nineveh was as wicked as it was impressive. The Assyrians were a notoriously brutal and wicked people. Assyrian kings boasted of the horrific ways in which they massacred their enemies and mutilated their captives—from dismemberment to decapitation to burning prisoners alive to other indescribably gory forms of torture. They posed a clear and present danger to the national security of Israel. Only a few decades after Jonah's mission, the Assyrians would conquer the northern tribes of Israel and take them into a captivity (in 722 BC), from which they would never return.

Jonah, who ministered in the northern kingdom of Israel during the reign of King Jeroboam II (ca. 793–758 BC), had prophesied that the borders of Israel would be restored through the military victories of their king (2 Kings 14:25). To subsequently take a message of repentance and hope to Israel's hated pagan enemies was unthinkable. The Assyrians were a civilization of murderous terrorists bent on the violent annihilation of all who stood in their path. If anyone deserved God's judgment, thought Jonah and the Israelites, it was the Ninevites. They were not worthy of divine compassion and forgiveness.

Of course, God was fully aware of Nineveh's iniquity. In fact, a century after Jonah and the repentance of the Ninevites, the Lord would condemn a subsequent generation in that same city through the prophet Nahum for its arrogance, deception, idolatry, sensuality, and violence. But before dispensing His wrath on that future generation, God determined to first offer the people of Nineveh mercy and forgiveness through repentance and trust in Him. Jonah was commissioned to deliver that message.

But the rebellious prophet did not want to see Israel's enemies receive mercy. He knew the Lord would forgive the Ninevites if they repented. And he hated that thought (cf. Jonah 4:2). So he determined not to offer that message to them and boarded a boat heading west.

Jonah's hatred of sinners, regardless of how he rationalized it, put him in a dangerous position. As a prophet of God, he surely knew his duty—but he would rather take the chastening of the Lord (seeing it as the lesser evil) than be instrumental in Gentile conversions. That is a bizarre perspective for a preacher! Perhaps he also thought that by going far enough away, in the opposite direction, he would no longer be available for the task, and God would have to find someone else to go to Nineveh. He could not have been more wrong.

ISRAEL: A NATION OF MISSIONARIES

Though this reluctant disobedience was the case with this one man, it was a symptom of a national failure of epic proportions. When Jonah rebelled against the Lord's command and ran in the opposite direction, he epitomized the collective failure of the nation of Israel to fulfill her God-given mission. From the beginning, the Lord elected Israel to be a nation of missionaries. As His chosen people, they were to be a light to the Gentiles—a people so passionate in their devotion to the Lord and zealous for other nations to love and worship the true God that their corporate testimony would reverberate throughout the world.

From within Israel, the Lord selected special men to be His prophets and to lead the missionary task. He called them to confront Israel's apathy and also to proclaim a message of repentance to the surrounding nations, warning them of God's pending judgment. A survey of Isaiah through Malachi reveals that the prophets did not merely focus their attention on the responsibilities of the people of Israel and Judah. They also addressed Ammon, Assyria, Babylon, Edom, Egypt, Elam, Hazor, Kedar, Medo-Persia, Moab, Philistia, Phoenicia, Syria, Tyre, and all unrepentant Gentiles. For the most part, the Hebrew prophets ministered within the borders of Israel and Judah—even while they gave warnings to other nations. But Jonah's calling was unique. He was commanded to travel far beyond the borders of Israel and preach to the Assyrians in their capital city.

Though the true prophets ministered faithfully, the people of Israel as a whole had rejected their God-appointed preachers and failed in their missionary task. Far from fulfilling their evangelistic mandate to the nations around them, they had even become arrogant and apathetic in their own faith and worship. Thus, the Lord's command to Jonah to go and preach repentance to Nineveh was more than just a missionary assignment. Jonah was sent to Nineveh in part to shame Israel by the fact that a pagan city would repent at the preaching of one stranger, whereas Israel would not repent and obey God though preached to by many prophets. The fact that the Ninevites responded, while Israel walked in stubborn unbelief, was a stinging rebuke to God's chosen nation. Centuries later, Jesus Himself would similarly use the Ninevites to admonish the unbelieving Pharisees of His day. The heathen city of Nineveh repented at the preaching of a reluctant prophet, but the Pharisees refused to repent at the preaching of the greatest of all prophets, in spite of overwhelming evidence that He was actually their Lord and Messiah.

Though most Christians know the names of the Hebrew Prophets, such as Jeremiah, Ezekiel, Hosea, and Joel, the prophetic books of the Old Testament represent some of the most unfamiliar territory in all the Bible. The Minor Prophets (Hosea through Malachi) in particular are often a neglected part of the Bible for many believers. (They are named "minor" prophets because of their relative brevity, not because they are less important than the other prophetic books.) Jonah is the one minor prophet that everyone knows about. Even unbelievers have heard his amazing story.

To be sure, Jonah's example is largely negative—meaning that he illustrates what not to do. This backward, grudging prophet, through his recalcitrant attitude and actions, provides for us a vivid picture of ministry gone wrong in the extreme. Most people would think he should have been permanently discarded and never heard from again! Yet God worked through him to conduct a campaign of preaching that brought hundreds of thousands to salvation. And that is what fits him into the list of heroes.

The book of Jonah teaches us that even when the preacher is reluctant to see sinners saved, God is not reluctant to save them. The Lord's compassion for the heathen was set on clear display as a striking contrast to Jonah's callous diffidence.

MAN OVERBOARD

Jonah's attempt to run from God did not end well for the recalcitrant missionary. Spiritual rebellion reaps what it sows, as God reproves and corrects those whom He loves (Hebrews 12:6). In Jonah's case, that correction came swiftly and in dramatic fashion—as his Tarshish-bound vessel was suddenly engulfed by a furious storm.

After identifying Jonah as the target of the storm, the frightened sailors looked to him for a way to appease his angry God.

> Then they said to him, "What shall we do to you that the sea may be calm for us?"—for the sea was growing more tempestuous. And he said to them, "Pick me up and throw me into the sea; then the sea will become calm for you. For I know that this great tempest is because of me." (Jonah 1:11–12)

God would have been pleased if the prophet had fallen to his knees in repentance and promised to head back to Nineveh. Such a response surely would have stopped the waves. Jonah, however, stubbornly demanded to be thrown into the sea. In effect, he was saying he would rather die than fulfill his mission to the Ninevites. Sadly, the pagan sailors showed a lot more compassion to Jonah than he displayed toward the Assyrians. Rather than immediately tossing him overboard in hope of ending the danger, they attempted to fight the waves and row the ship to shore. Though kindly motivated, their efforts failed. With no other options, they submitted to Jonah's request and

> . . . cried out to the Lord and said, "We pray, O Lord, please do not let us perish for this man's life, and do not charge us with innocent blood; for You, O Lord, have done as it pleased You." So they picked up Jonah and threw him into the sea, and the sea ceased from its raging. (vv. 14–15)

The supernatural character of the raging storm became immediately apparent as soon as Jonah hit the water—the wind instantly stopped and the massive waves flattened! The astonished sailors responded in reverent awe and repentant faith, "Then the men feared the Lord exceedingly, and offered a sacrifice to the Lord and took vows" (v. 16). Despite Jonah's determined disobedience, God used him to display His power to a crew of Gentile seamen. The Lord would do the same for Nineveh—reaching that pagan population and bringing them to penitent faith by the same reluctant preacher.

Jonah was gone, and so was the storm. As he slipped beneath the ocean's surface, the suicidal castaway surely thought he had escaped his unwanted mission. But the Lord was not done with him yet. Rather than allowing him to drown, "the LORD had prepared a great fish to swallow Jonah. And Jonah was in the belly of the fish three days and three nights" (v. 17).

FROM THE BELLY OF THE FISH

Though it has been highly romanticized as a Sunday school classic, Jonah's three-day stay inside a fish was an indescribable horror. Lodged in the cramped and clammy darkness, he was likely unable to move and barely able to breathe due to the suffocating stench. The gastric acids of the fish's stomach ate away at his skin, and the constant motion of the fish combined with the changing pressure of the ocean's depths must have been absolutely nauseating. Though attempts have been made to provide a scientific explanation for Jonah's survival, it is best to understand this remarkable preservation as a divine miracle. The Lord prepared the fish to swallow Jonah, and He protected Jonah supernaturally. (Because the Hebrew word for *whale* is not used, Jonah's host was likely not a warm-blooded mammal—making his agonies in the cold wetness all the more unimaginable.)

In the midst of his misery, the humbled prophet cried out for deliverance. His prayer of repentance, recorded in Jonah 2, is one of the most poignant in all of Scripture, a cry out of suffocating circumstances:

> *I cried out to the LORD because of my affliction,*
> *And He answered me.*

Out of the belly of Sheol I cried,
And You heard my voice.
For You cast me into the deep,
Into the heart of the seas,
And the floods surrounded me;
All Your billows and Your waves passed over me.
Then I said, "I have been cast out of Your sight;
Yet I will look again toward Your holy temple."
The waters surrounded me, even to my soul;
The deep closed around me;
Weeds were wrapped around my head.
I went down to the moorings of the mountains;
The earth with its bars closed behind me forever;
Yet You have brought up my life from the pit,
O LORD, my God.
When my soul fainted within me,
I remembered the LORD;
And my prayer went up to You,
Into Your holy temple.
Those who regard worthless idols
Forsake their own Mercy.
But I will sacrifice to You
With the voice of thanksgiving;
I will pay what I have vowed.
Salvation is of the LORD. (Jonah 2:2–9)

The man who recoiled at the thought of God extending mercy to Assyria begged the Lord for grace and compassion from the depths of his own desperation. And God graciously answered his prayer.

Jonah's prayer indicates that he sank far below the surface before being swallowed. His reference to "Sheol" does not necessarily mean that he died, but more likely refers to the catastrophic circumstances surrounding his near-death experience. It was there, submerged in the ocean deep, that Jonah cried out for the God he was running from to come to him. He acknowledged both the Lord's powerful presence (in verses 1–6) and His saving grace (in verses 7–9). Drowning under the weight of God's hand of judgment, Jonah prayed for deliverance and compassion from the Judge Himself.

Three days later, a wet, disheveled, and slime-covered prophet collapsed with a stench onto the sandy beach. He had just been violently expelled from his gastric prison by a fish that had endured three days of indigestion so that the Lord could teach Jonah a lesson. But the rebel prophet had repented. When the word of the Lord came to Jonah a second time, he would be sure to obey.

JONAH GOES TO "FISH TOWN"

The Lord's compassion toward Jonah not only resulted in the prophet's rescue but also in his restoration to ministry usefulness. In Jonah 1:2, God had commissioned the prophet to go to Nineveh, but Jonah disobeyed. Two chapters (and several traumatic events) later, the Lord issued the same command again: "Arise, go to Nineveh, that great city, and preach to it the message that I tell you" (Jonah 3:2). This time Jonah fully submitted, traveling east to the Assyrian capital.

Nineveh was settled on the banks of the Tigris River approximately five hundred miles northeast of Israel. According to historians, magnificent walls almost eight miles long enveloped the inner city, with the rest of the city and surrounding district occupying an area with a circumference of some sixty miles. The name Nineveh is thought to derive from *ninus* (for Nimrod, the city's founder) and means the residence of Nimrod or *nunu*, which is Akkadian for *fish*. Thus, the city's name could be reduced to "fish town." Moreover, the people worshiped the fish goddess Nanshe (the daughter of Ea, the goddess of fresh water) and the fish god Dagon, a statue of a man with a fish head. As these examples indicate, fish were of particular significance to the Ninevites—which likely explains why they took such great interest in Jonah and his fish story when he first arrived in the city. (It has even been suggested that acids from the fish's stomach bleached Jonah's skin so that he arrived in Nineveh with a distinctly white, almost ghostly appearance.)

Jonah's message was far more than a fish story. It was a threat: "Yet forty days, and Nineveh shall be overthrown!" (Jonah 3:4). What happened next was a far more extreme and amazing miracle than the supernatural storm and the prophet-swallowing fish had been. The text declares the miracle in a seriously understated way: "the people of Nineveh believed God" (Jonah 3:5). Those few words describe the largest scale revival recorded in the Old Testament, as the entire population of Nineveh—numbering in the hundreds of thousands—repented and turned to the Lord.

What made the Ninevites so receptive to Jonah's message? Some scholars have suggested that military defeats or civil unrest or natural phenomena (like earthquakes and eclipses) may have preconditioned the people so that they were ready to receive the prophet's warning. In reality, however, there is no natural explanation for such a massive conversion. There is, however, a supernatural explanation: the Lord went before Jonah and prepared the hearts of the Ninevites. To accomplish His sovereign saving purpose, He used a rebellious prophet to bring rebellious people to faith in Himself.

The full extent of their repentance is explained in Jonah 3:5–9. Everyone in the city, including the king himself, responded with heartfelt sorrow:

> So the people of Nineveh believed God, proclaimed a fast, and put on sackcloth, from the greatest to the least of them. Then word came to the king of Nineveh; and he arose from his throne and laid aside his robe, covered himself with sackcloth and sat in ashes. And he caused it to be proclaimed and published throughout Nineveh by the decree of the king and his nobles, saying,

Let neither man nor beast, herd nor flock, taste anything; do not let them eat, or drink water. But let man and beast be covered with sackcloth, and cry mightily to God; yes, let every one turn from his evil way and from the violence that is in his hands. Who can tell if God will turn and relent, and turn away from His fierce anger, so that we may not perish?

The king, likely identified as either Adad-nirari III (ca. 810–783 BC) or Assurdan III (ca. 772–755 BC), exchanged his royal robes for sackcloth and ashes. In a public display of personal mourning and to symbolize national repentance, the Assyrian monarch pled to the true God for mercy and forgiveness. Just as He had done for Jonah, the Lord answered the king's prayer. "Then God saw their works, that they turned from their evil way; and God relented from the disaster that He had said He would bring upon them, and He did not do it" (v. 10).

Such astounding impact on an entire nation by a deeply flawed prophet who repented is a classic example of God's grace in making heroes out of unlikely people.

JONAH'S ANGRY REACTION

Most missionaries would be extremely elated by such an overwhelming response to their message. Not Jonah. His attitude of prejudicial hatred toward the Assyrians was still firmly embedded. If the people of Nineveh repented, it meant they would not be judged. And this zealous Israelite was not happy about that prospect:

But it displeased Jonah exceedingly, and he became angry. So he prayed to the LORD, and said, "Ah, LORD, was not this what I said when I was still in my country? Therefore I fled previously to Tarshish; for I know that You are a gracious and merciful God, slow to anger and abundant in lovingkindness, One who relents from doing harm. Therefore now, O LORD, please take my life from me, for it is better for me to die than to live!" (Jonah 4:1–3)

Incredibly, Jonah would have preferred death over the salvation of his enemies! No wonder he fled toward Tarshish, fell asleep in the midst of a storm, and volunteered to be thrown overboard. Given the choice, Jonah would rather be killed than preach to the Ninevites! But Jonah's rebellion could not overturn the sovereign grace of God; the Lord used Jonah to accomplish His saving purposes in spite of the prophet's petty protests.

Jonah's prayer not only exposed his own prejudice and pride, but also showcased the lovingkindness and compassion of God. In His infinite mercy and grace, the Lord can rescue any sinner, even one as wicked as the pagan king of a barbarian nation. Jonah recognized the magnitude of God's grace, which is why he initially ran in the opposite direction; he wanted nothing to do with divine pardon being extended to Israel's hostile enemies. Ironically, when Jonah himself was in trouble, he cried out for God's mercy. But when the Lord extended grace to others, Jonah was filled with resentment. When God withheld His wrath from the Ninevites, the prophet's wrath was aroused.

In annoyed disbelief—angered that his prophetic mission had been so stunningly successful—Jonah set up camp on the outskirts of Nineveh to see if perhaps God would still judge the city. Evidently, he hoped that the people's repentance would prove to be hypocritical and superficial so that the Lord would still destroy them after forty days. The prophet hastily constructed a temporary shelter to shade him from the blazing sun and waited to see how it all played out.

A FINAL OBJECT LESSON

As Jonah sat disgruntled in his lean-to shanty on the eastern edge of Nineveh, the Lord graciously caused a large plant to instantly grow up behind him, providing the melancholy prophet some shady relief from the beating Assyrian sun. The type of plant is uncertain, though it could have been the fast growing castor oil plant, which in hot climates grows rapidly and gives shade with its unusually large leaves. Whatever the variety, this leafy vegetation grew *miraculously* fast, immediately covering Jonah's inadequate shelter and providing him cover from the direct sun.

The text states that Jonah was thankful for the plant. But the next morning, when God sent a worm to eat the plant, the prophet's anger was again incited. The situation worsened when the Lord sent a scorching east wind (called a "sirocco"), which overwhelmed Jonah's makeshift shelter and brought him to the point of extreme heat exposure. In the same way that God had hurled a great wind on the sea to affect Jonah (1:4), He prepared this hot desert wind for the same purpose—to humble His servant and teach him a vital spiritual lesson.

And true to form, the whining, faithless prophet once again wished for death. As He had all along, the Lord responded to him with undeserved patience:

> Then God said to Jonah, "Is it right for you to be angry about the plant?" And he said, "It is right for me to be angry, even to death!" But the LORD said, "You have had pity on the plant for which you have not labored, nor made it grow, which came up in a night and perished in a night. And should I not pity Nineveh, that great city, in which are more than one hundred and twenty thousand persons who cannot discern between their right hand and their left—and much livestock?" (Jonah 4:9–11)

Jonah's perspective was completely backward and entirely self-centered. He was passionately concerned about a short-lived shade plant to protect himself from discomfort, but had no compassion for the entire population of Nineveh, including one hundred twenty thousand small children (those who cannot discern between their right and left hands). They were headed to eternal punishment if they did not repent. But Jonah was so stubbornly calloused that he was not merely indifferent to their eternal danger, he *wanted* to see them judged. In his contempt, he would gladly have let God condemn a whole city of people to hell. The self-centered prophet was saying, in essence, "Save the plant for my temporary relief, but sentence the people to everlasting torment." But God's love for the Ninevites was markedly different than Jonah's warped disdain.

The stubborn, prejudiced prophet had been operating in his own self-interest, but the Lord wanted him to put the eternally significant message of salvation above his own myopic concerns and trivial comforts. How could he be concerned about a weed when hundreds of thousands of souls faced judgment and he had the opportunity to see them saved?

The book of Jonah ends abruptly, with those final words from the Lord forming its sudden conclusion. But the lesson for Jonah was unmistakably clear, and that same lesson is vitally important for all believers to learn. Like Jonah, we might be tempted to allow our own fears, prejudices, or selfish interests to inhibit our gospel witness. But when we prioritize the gospel message over our own personal agendas, we bring glory to God as we advance His kingdom purposes throughout the world.

WHAT JONAH TEACHES US ABOUT GOD

Like all of the biblical accounts we've studied so far, the story of Jonah is *primarily* about God. He is the ultimate hero of the story—the One who saves Nineveh in spite of the rebellious prophet's attempts to thwart the mission. Though the book is relatively short, it nonetheless unfolds three profound and unforgettable truths about the character of God.

First, the story of Jonah emphasizes the fact that God is the sovereign Creator. Throughout the entire narrative, the reader is continually reminded that the Lord is controlling all of Jonah's circumstances. It is God who sends the wind, incites the storm, calms the seas, prepares the fish, grows the plant, sends the worm, and then whips up the wind once again. The pagan sailors recognize the Lord's power over creation and worship Him as a result. The pagan king of Nineveh likewise recognizes God's sovereign hand. Surprisingly, the only person who resists God is Jonah—the prophet of Israel who acknowledged the Lord's sovereignty with his lips (Jonah 1:9) yet rebelled against it with his life.

Second, the Jonah account reminds us that God is the supreme Judge. That, in fact, was the message the prophet was to deliver to the Assyrians. After forty days, their city would become the object of divine wrath. But God's judgment never came upon the people of Nineveh. Instead, it came only in the form of chastisement against Jonah for his deliberate disobedience. Recognizing that their doom was imminent, the Ninevites repented, and God's wrath against them was withheld.

Finally, Jonah's story reiterates the fact that God is the Savior and that His lovingkindness is not limited by our prejudicial preconceptions. The prophet Jonah considered the Assyrians beyond the reach of God's mercy. After all, they were the brutal, idolatrous, Gentile enemies of Israel and Israel's God! But the Lord showed Jonah that His saving grace extends to all who repent and believe in Him. In this way, the book of Jonah encapsulates the message of salvation. When sinners recognize the Lord as Sovereign Creator and Judge of the Universe, and cry out to Him for mercy, He graciously saves them from divine wrath, giving them eternal life instead.

Those three truths point to the heart of the gospel. Sinners are creatures who have broken God's law. They await His wrath, yet He offers them forgiveness and salvation through the sacrifice of His Son, Jesus Christ. Jesus Himself used the prophet Jonah, and the three days he spent in the belly of the fish, as an illustration of His own death and resurrection. In Matthew 12:40, Jesus told the crowd who had gathered, "For as Jonah was three days and three nights in the belly of the great fish, so will the Son of Man be three days and three nights in the heart of the earth." Three days after He was crucified, Christ rose triumphant from the grave, demonstrating once and for all that He is the Savior of the world. Those who repent from their sin and believe in Him, whether Jew or Gentile, will be saved (Romans 10:9–10).

Although we are not Old Testament prophets like Jonah was, we have been given a mission similar to his. As New Testament believers, our charge is to take the gospel to those who are lost, proclaiming to them the reality of coming judgment and the hope of salvation (cf. Matthew 28:18–20). When we resist this responsibility, whether out of fear, pride, or a preoccupation with trivial things, we fall into the same trap that Jonah did. But when we are faithful to obey the Lord in this way, we experience the wonderful blessing of being used by Him to further His kingdom. There is no greater joy than seeing sinners embrace the good news of salvation. As the apostle Paul told the Romans, quoting from Isaiah, "How beautiful are the feet of those who preach the gospel of peace, who bring glad tidings of good things!" (Romans 10:15).

7

ESTHER: FOR SUCH A
TIME AS THIS

—⁓—

Then Esther told them to reply to Mordecai: "Go, gather all the Jews who are present in Shushan, and fast for me; neither eat nor drink for three days, night or day. My maids and I will fast likewise. And so I will go to the king, which is against the law; and if I perish, I perish!"

—ESTHER 4:15–16

THE YEAR WAS 480 BC. A massive Persian army marched with untiring determination to face the rebel forces of Athens and its Greek allies. Ancient sources number the Persian host in the millions of men; modern scholars believe it was probably in the hundreds of thousands. In any case, it was an impressive display of military might.

At that time, the Persian (or Achaemenid) Empire stretched from modern-day Libya in Africa to Pakistan in Asia. It was the largest empire in history up to that point, with about fifty million people residing within its borders. After having conquered the Babylonian (Chaldean) empire in 539 BC, the Persians settled into domination over the Middle Eastern world for two centuries.

Initially, regions of Greece had been conquered by the Persians under Darius I (550–486 BC). But Darius's armies had been defeated by the Athenians at the famous battle of Marathon in 490 BC. Enraged and undeterred, Darius was determined to subdue his Greek enemies. Returning home, he began to amass a great army, but died before he was able to satisfy his thirst for vengeance.

The quest for revenge fell to his son, Xerxes I (519–465 BC), who rose to power in 486. Upon taking the throne, the new ruler faced rebellions within his empire, from Egypt and Babylon, which he effectively subdued. Xerxes, engaged with the revolts, was unable to immediately set his sights on Greece, but by 481 he was ready to attack. His force of two hundred fifty thousand was stationed in modern-day Turkey, waiting for orders to cross into Greece. Eager to avenge his father's honor and proud of his power, Xerxes was confident of victory, especially since his army heavily outnumbered the enemy.

But things did not go as Xerxes expected. Though his armies reached Athens and sacked the city, the Greeks ultimately defeated the Persians (in 479) and drove them out of Greece. Several dramatic battles made the unexpected Greek victory legendary. At the famous Battle of Thermopylae (in 480), a relatively small force of Greek soldiers was able to hold off the much larger Persian army for several days until their position was flanked and they were forced to retreat. In order to safeguard the retreating Greek army, a group of three hundred Spartans and several hundred others stayed behind and fought to the death. Their courageous last stand immediately became a rallying cry for the larger Greek cause and an iconic story of heroism throughout history. Even in modern times, the battle's climactic end has been immortalized in songs, speeches, literary works, and films.

A month after Thermopylae, the Persian navy—which consisted of hundreds of warships—suffered a major defeat at the Battle of Salamis. Knowing they were outnumbered, the Greeks lured the Persians into the narrow straits of Salamis. In the cramped waterways, the size of the bulky Persian navy proved to be a major disadvantage as their fleet became unmanageable and disorganized. The Greeks pounced on the advantage and destroyed some three hundred enemy vessels.

With much of his navy sunk, the vanquished Xerxes was forced to flee back to Persia with most of his army. He left his general, Mardonius, behind in Greece to continue fighting, though with a much smaller number of soldiers. Those remaining Persian forces were finally defeated by the Greeks in August 479 at the Battle of Plataea. Against great odds, the Athenians and their allies vanquished a much larger invading army. Their victory marked a major turning point in the Greco-Persian wars and shaped the history of western civilization by pushing the balance of power toward Greece. Under Alexander the Great, one hundred fifty years later, the Persian Empire was defeated for good.

But what does all this ancient history have to do with the biblical story of Esther? The emperor whom the Greeks called *Xerxes* was known in Persia as *Khsayarsha*, and in Hebrew as *Achashverosh*. Our English Bibles transliterate his name as *Ahasuerus*. He is the very king featured in the book of Esther! In God's perfect providence, the man who tried to conquer Greece with at least a quarter-of-a-million soldiers—the ruler of the most powerful empire in the world at that time—that man would find his heart conquered by the charm and beauty of a Jewish orphan girl named Esther. When the opportunity came, she would use her influence with the king to save her people from annihilation.

The book that bears her name was not written by Esther, but about her. Maybe the author the Holy Spirit used was her relative Mordecai, or Ezra, or Nehemiah, or another Jew dwelling in Persia. Whoever wrote this history possessed a detailed knowledge of Persian customs and history, as well as Jewish features, including a strong sense of Jewish nationalism. That all plays richly into the remarkable labyrinth of this story.

THE FIRST QUEEN IS DEPOSED

The book opens by describing the expansive kingdom of Ahasuerus—noting that the Persian Empire extended from Ethiopia to the western edges of India. Ahasuerus was the grandson of Cyrus the Great (ca. 600–530 BC), the Persian ruler who allowed the Jews to return home after seventy years of captivity in Babylon (cf. Ezra 1:1–4). Though many Jews went back to Israel at that time, many remained settled and scattered throughout the Persian Empire.

Several years into his reign, Ahasuerus summoned the princes and nobles of Persia to attend a six-month summit in the capital city of Shushan, also called Susa (Esther 1:3–4). This gathering, which occurred in 483 BC, was undoubtedly a strategic war-planning meeting—during which the king and his royal advisors made final preparations for the aforementioned invasion into Greece. Confident that his military forces would be triumphant, Ahasuerus concluded the summit with a seven-day banquet for the entire city of Shushan. Esther 1:6–7 describes the extravagant celebration of the anticipated victory:

> There were white and blue linen curtains fastened with cords of fine linen and purple on silver rods and marble pillars; and the couches were of gold and silver on a mosaic pavement of alabaster, turquoise, and white and black marble. And they served drinks in golden vessels, each vessel being different from the other, with royal wine in abundance, according to the generosity of the king.

On the seventh day of the feast, Ahasuerus (after a week of indulgence and intoxication) commanded his wife, Queen Vashti (whose Greek name was *Amestris*), to appear before his nobles in all her royal regalia. Surprisingly, Vashti refused, evidently concerned that her dignity would be tarnished by appearing before a crowd of drunken onlookers. It is also possible that the queen was pregnant with their son, Artaxerxes, and was therefore uncomfortable to be seen in public. Whatever his wife's excuse might have been, Ahasuerus was furious when he heard she was unwilling to obey him and appear for all his guests.

After discussing the public insubordination and embarrassment with his royal advisors, who also feared that the queen's actions might spark a women's liberation movement (cf. Esther 1:17–18), Ahasuerus decided to demote Vashti and find himself a new queen. As was customary in Persian law, the king announced his intentions by issuing an unalterable decree. It was sent to every corner of the Persian Empire, declaring that because Vashti had disobeyed the king, her exalted position would be given to someone more deserving of it. Though harsh, Ahasuerus was making his point unmistakably clear: no one, not even the queen, could refuse a royal order and get away with it.

As his response to Vashti demonstrates, Ahasuerus had a violent temper. Just a year later, in order for his massive army to march from modern-day Turkey into Greece, Ahasuerus ordered bridges built across the Hellespont, the narrow strait of water that runs from the Black Sea to the Mediterranean. But when the bridges were destroyed in a storm before the troops were able to cross, Ahasuerus became infuriated. According to the ancient Greek historian Herodotus, the Persian emperor ordered the engineers who designed the bridges to be beheaded. He then sent soldiers into the water with whips, demanding that they lash the ocean three hundred times for its insubordination! His soldiers also threw shackles into the water and stabbed the waves with red-hot branding irons—all to soothe the king's arrogant and irrational rage.

Vashti and everyone else learned that violating the will of the imperial dictator could have very serious consequences.

A NEW QUEEN IS CHOSEN

According to Esther 2:16, four years passed before Ahasuerus got around to selecting a new queen. Even with all the necessary preparations, a new queen could have easily been enthroned within two years. So why did it take Ahasuerus so long to select Vashti's replacement?

The answer is found in Persia's two-year, unsuccessful invasion of Greece, which historically fits right between Vashti's demotion (in 483 or 482 BC) and Esther's coronation (in 479 or 478). As noted earlier, Ahasuerus himself returned to Persia in 480, before the war was over. Frustrated by the situation in Greece, the king came back to his capital at Shushan, only to face the reality that he had no queen. With the war effort going badly, Ahasuerus needed a distraction. Selecting a new queen was the perfect diversion. As Esther 2:1–4 explains,

> After these things, when the wrath of King Ahasuerus subsided, he remembered Vashti, what she had done, and what had been decreed against her. Then the king's servants who attended him said: "Let beautiful young virgins be sought for the king; and let the king appoint officers in all the provinces of his kingdom, that they may gather all the beautiful young virgins to Shushan the citadel, into the women's quarters, under the custody of Hegai the king's eunuch, custodian of the women. And let beauty preparations be given them. Then let the young woman who pleases the king be queen instead of Vashti." This thing pleased the king, and he did so.

At this point the biblical text introduces us to the two main people of the book of Esther—two Jewish cousins who were living in the city of Shushan. They were descendants of Jewish captives who had been taken from Jerusalem by Nebuchadnezzar and brought to Babylon over a century earlier, around 597 BC (cf. Esther 2:6). The older of the two, a man named Mordecai, was roughly fifteen years older than his younger cousin, an orphan named Esther. Because Esther's parents had died when she was very young, Mordecai had raised her as his own daughter (v. 7).

Esther's Hebrew name, *Hadassah*, means "myrtle." Her Persian name, *Esther*, probably came from the Persian word for "star," though it may have been derived from Ishtar, the Babylonian goddess of love. (It was common for Jews outside of Israel to receive a second, pagan name—as evidenced by Daniel and his three friends (Daniel 1:7).) The biblical text describes the young virgin as "lovely and beautiful" (Esther 2:7). And her external beauty did not go unnoticed by the king's officials, so she was taken to the palace to live with the other beauties in the contest for queen.

According to Josephus, the first-century Jewish historian, four hundred virgins were selected as queen candidates from among the twenty-five million women who lived in the empire. After making all the appropriate preparations, each maiden would be individually presented to Ahasuerus. They would all then be assigned to the king's harem, while one would be elevated to queen (cf. Esther 2:14).

There was a year of beautification and primping leading to the final preparation when a virgin would go before the emperor, not only looking as pretty as possible, but also smelling good—with the aid of incense and cosmetic burners in order to enhance the skin and hair with pleasant fragrances. Special instruction was also given regarding the etiquette of the imperial court and especially expectations for royal concubines. In the end, twelve months of intensive preparation came down to one opportunity to impress the king. For that all-important encounter, each young lady was allowed to adorn herself with whatever apparel or jewelry she desired. She would then be presented to the ruler. The day after, she would join the other concubines in another part of the palace. There she would wait indefinitely as a member of the royal harem, hoping the king would choose her from among the four hundred.

Esther was likely in her twenties when, after completing the year-long ordeal, she appeared before Ahasuerus. According to Esther 2:16–18:

So Esther was taken to King Ahasuerus, into his royal palace, in the tenth month, which is the month of Tebeth, in the seventh year of his reign. The king loved Esther more than all the other women, and she obtained grace and favor in his sight more than all the virgins; so he set the royal crown upon her head and made her queen instead of Vashti. Then the king made a great feast, the Feast of Esther, for all his officials and servants; and he proclaimed a holiday in the provinces and gave gifts according to the generosity of a king.

Like an ancient Cinderella story, Esther stole the king's heart and became his queen! Thus, an obscure Jewish orphan girl was exalted to the highest position of any woman in the world at that time. Out of the twenty-five million women in the empire, it had come down to Esther being singled out by the king himself. This was clearly no coincidence. A Power infinitely greater than Ahasuerus was at work, providentially orchestrating His purposes through the emperor's affections.

Significantly, throughout the entire process, Esther kept her Jewish identity a secret—just as Mordecai instructed her to do. This was likely due to the strong anti-Semitism that existed in the Persian Empire at that time (cf. Ezra 4:6). Esther would reveal her ethnic heritage, but not until the situation left her with no option.

MORDECAI FOILS A SINISTER PLOT

One day, not long after Esther was crowned, her cousin Mordecai was sitting at the entrance to the palace. There he evidently overheard a plot to assassinate Ahasuerus. As the text explains, "Two of the king's eunuchs, Bigthan and Teresh, doorkeepers, became furious and sought to lay hands on King Ahasuerus" (Esther 2:21). These royal officials likely guarded the king's private quarters and may have been angry because of loyalty to the recently disgraced

Queen Vashti. They had the motive and needed only the opportunity to make an attempt on the emperor's life.

The fact that Mordecai had such inside access to the private places in the palace suggests that he himself held an official position of prominence in the imperial government. When he learned of the plot against the king, he reported it immediately. According to vv. 22–23:

> So the matter became known to Mordecai, who told Queen Esther, and Esther informed the king in Mordecai's name. And when an inquiry was made into the matter, it was confirmed, and both were hanged on a gallows; and it was written in the book of the chronicles in the presence of the king.

Importantly, Mordecai's actions were written down in the royal records—which would be used in a future day as the basis of his being rewarded by the king. Like all ancient monarchs, Ahasuerus was careful to honor and reward those who demonstrated their loyalty to him. Thus it was required to keep a record of notable acts of valor and special service rendered to the Persian monarch. According to Herodotus, the ancient Greek historian, Ahasuerus would even do this in the midst of battle. "Whenever Xerxes [Ahasuerus] . . . saw one of his own men achieve some feat in the battle, he inquired who did it, and his scribes wrote down the captain's name with his father and city of residence" (*Histories*, 8.90.4). The record of the brave soldier would lead to an appropriate honor for his loyal service.

HAMAN HATCHES A DIABOLICAL PLAN

In the third chapter of Esther, we are introduced to the villain Haman, a man whom the king had exalted above his other princes and royal officials. From his introduction on, we are reminded that Haman was an Agagite—a designation repeated throughout the book (3:1, 10; 8:3, 5; 9:24). That he was an Agagite is no small detail. It is the origin of Haman's deep resentment toward the Jews and his effort to eliminate them.

To get the point, we need to understand that the hostility between the Agagites and the Jews went back almost a thousand years to the exodus from Egypt (around 1445 BC) when the Israelites were attacked by the Amalekites (Exodus 17:8–16), who were descendants of Esau. For that attack, God cursed the Amalekites, prophesying that one day they would become extinct (Deuteronomy 25:17–19). Four centuries later, King Saul conquered the Amalekites and captured their king, whose name was Agag (1 Samuel 15:2–3). As we saw in chapter 5, Saul had been ordered to kill Agag; but he disobeyed, letting him live, and incurred the Lord's displeasure. The prophet Samuel finally executed God's command and hacked the pagan Amalekite King Agag to death (1 Samuel 15:32–33).

Haman was a descendant of Agag, who carried long-nurtured feelings of intense hatred toward the Israelites because they had defeated the Amalekites and put Agag to death. The plot thickens when we realize, also, that Mordecai was a descendant of Kish (Esther 2:5), a man from the tribe of Benjamin, who was from the line of Saul. Though five hundred fifty years had passed since Saul and Agag, neither Haman the Agagite nor Mordecai, the Benjamite descendant of Saul, had forgotten the tribal feud that still smoldered deep beneath the surface.

That hostility erupted when the two men met:

All the king's servants who were within the king's gate bowed and paid homage to Haman, for so the king had commanded concerning him. But Mordecai would not bow or pay homage. . . . When Haman saw that Mordecai did not bow or pay him homage, Haman was filled with wrath. But he disdained to lay hands on Mordecai alone, for they had told him of the people of Mordecai. Instead, Haman sought to destroy all the Jews who were throughout the whole kingdom of Ahasuerus—the people of Mordecai. (Esther 3:2, 5–6)

The generational hostility between the Amalekites and the Israelites explains why Mordecai refused to bow down to Haman, and why Haman responded by viciously plotting not only to kill Mordecai, but to exterminate the entire Jewish population.

Full of anger, Haman sought the advice of Persian magicians and astrologers, who cast lots to determine the optimum day on which to annihilate the Jewish people. He then went to the king and deceitfully misrepresented the Jews as a rebellious threat to the empire that needed to be eliminated. Haman proposed that all Jews living within the Persian Empire ought to be killed (including those who had returned to the land of Israel). In order to sweeten his proposition, Haman promised that—by destroying the Jews—a vast sum of money would come into the royal treasury from the spoils they left. Trusting the advice of his chief courtier, and falsely thinking he was going to squelch a rebellion before it began, Ahasuerus gave his signet ring to Haman and told him to use it to authorize the genocide.

Haman hit the fast track, dispatching a royal decree throughout the entire Persian Empire that set aside a day, eleven months later, for one deadly purpose: "to destroy, to kill, and to annihilate all the Jews, both young and old, little children and women" (Esther 3:13). The Persian courier system operated like an ancient version of the Pony Express, as messengers rode from one outpost to the next. At each outpost, fresh horses and riders would be waiting to carry the message the next leg of the journey. Using this efficient system, royal decrees could rapidly reach all parts of the Persian Empire—in a matter of days. As the shocking news spread quickly, it brought down great distress and fear on the Jews throughout the empire. "In every province where the king's command and decree arrived, there was great mourning among the Jews, with fasting, weeping, and wailing; and many lay in sackcloth and ashes" (4:3).

MORDECAI PETITIONS THE QUEEN

When he heard about the genocidal decree, Mordecai tore his clothes, dressed himself in rags, poured ashes on his head, and mourned publicly. He must have been a spectacle, sitting outside the king's gate and wailing loudly. Undoubtedly, Mordecai realized that his earlier actions—refusing to bow down before Haman—contributed to this extermination as an act of retaliation. Haman's vengeful plan for the mass murder of the entire Jewish population, however, went far beyond a simple payback for Mordecai's disrespect. This was a much bigger scheme that involved Satan himself.

It did not take long for news to reach the ears of Esther that her older cousin was making a scene just outside the palace gates. The queen sent her servant Hathach to find out what was wrong. With dead seriousness, Mordecai informed Esther of what Haman had succeeded in accomplishing and sent Hathach back to her with a copy of the royal decree. He also urged her to plead with the king on behalf of the lives of the Jews.

Mordecai's plan for Esther's appeal sounded simple enough. But it was considerably more complicated. In Persia, no one, including the queen, could appear before the king without his express invitation. This helped to protect the emperor from unwanted intruders, which was an important precaution at a time when assassination attempts were not uncommon. If a would-be guest showed up uninvited, and the king did not extend his royal scepter as a sign of welcome, the intruder could be killed on the spot. In order to comply with Mordecai's request, Esther not only would be breaking royal protocol, but would risk her life. She explained that reality to her cousin,

> All the king's servants and the people of the king's provinces know
> that any man or woman who goes into the inner court to the king,
> who has not been called, he has but one law: put all to death,
> except the one to whom the king holds out the golden scepter, that

he may live. Yet I myself have not been called to go in to the king these thirty days. (Esther 4:11)

The queen was understandably afraid of her potentially violent and irrational husband, who had demoted and publicly disgraced Vashti for just one act of noncompliance. Mordecai was putting Esther in a position to disregard the law and approach the king uninvited. The fact that Ahasuerus had not called on her for thirty prior days only increased Esther's apprehensions. Perhaps she wondered if she had fallen out of his favor, or if his affection for her had turned to indifference, such that he would show her no mercy.

Mordecai's response urged Esther to be courageous given the seriousness of the situation. "Do not think in your heart that you will escape in the king's palace any more than all the other Jews," he warned his royal cousin. "For if you remain completely silent at this time, relief and deliverance will arise for the Jews from another place, but you and your father's house will perish. Yet who knows whether you have come to the kingdom for such a time as this?" (vv. 13–14). Mordecai's rhetorical question was an indirect affirmation of divine sovereignty, though he did not specifically mention God's involvement. He understood that Esther's placement in the palace was not the product of chance. In His purpose, God had given her a royal position for such a time as this.

Finally embracing her divinely granted role, Esther responded with courage and resolve:

Go, gather all the Jews who are present in Shushan, and fast for me; neither eat nor drink for three days, night or day. My maids and I will fast likewise. And so I will go to the king, which is against the law; and if I perish, I perish! (Esther 4:16)

Even if it cost her life, Esther would do whatever was necessary to protect her people. Though Esther's reply does not mention prayer, it was traditionally a part of any Jewish fast. So for three days, she and her fellow Jews prayed as she prepared herself to face the king.

Esther approached the throne tensely, wondering what the king's response would be; the seconds felt like hours as she waited for Ahasuerus to acknowledge her presence. Then it happened: he looked at her and extended his royal scepter to her, eagerly welcoming his beauty into his presence. To underscore his delight, the king responded with a question marked by generosity in typical royal hyperbole, "What do you wish, Queen Esther? What is your request? It shall be given to you—up to half the kingdom!" (Esther 5:3). She didn't want half the kingdom or any part of it. She wanted the lives of her people. So Esther's reply was a simple request that Ahasuerus and Haman join her for a banquet later that day. The king was both obligated by his pledge and delighted to be with her. As Esther 5:5–8 reports:

> So the king and Haman went to the banquet that Esther had prepared. At the banquet of wine the king said to Esther, "What is your petition? It shall be granted you. What is your request, up to half the kingdom? It shall be done!" Then Esther answered and said, "My petition and request is this: If I have found favor in the sight of the king, and if it pleases the king to grant my petition and fulfill my request, then let the king and Haman come to the banquet which I will prepare for them, and tomorrow I will do as the king has said."

Once again, the king's affection for Esther is clearly revealed in that he repeated his promise to give her whatever she wanted. And for a second time, the queen invited him and Haman to a banquet. Esther knew how critical it was that her real request be made when the timing was right. It appears the first feast was not the optimum time, so she decided to wait until the following day to petition the king on behalf of her people in the presence of their enemy, Haman.

HAMAN'S HATRED FOR
MORDECAI INTENSIFIES

Haman left the feast feeling confident about himself and his achievement. Not only had Ahasuerus exalted him above all the other princes and royal officials, but Queen Esther had invited him to not one, but two exclusive banquets as the guest of the royals. No higher honor could be given.

As Haman started back to his house, after the heady evening with the monarchs, he noticed Mordecai sitting at the king's gate. That sight triggered rage in his heart. Arriving at home, he gathered his family and friends and expressed his disdain toward Mordecai. They suggested a quick and easy remedy: erect gallows and have Mordecai executed in the morning. It seemed like a perfect solution to Haman, so he quickly had the gallows constructed.

That night, while Haman slept soundly and dreamt of his revenge, Ahasuerus tossed and turned, unable to sleep (cf. Esther 6:1). Perhaps he wondered as to the true nature of Queen Esther's request. Or perhaps some other imperial matter kept him awake. Whatever the cause of his insomnia, the king called for the royal records to be read to him. If anything could put him out for the night, it would be listening to the monotony of detailed government reports from the imperial archives.

The Persians kept extensive records, so it was only by the hand of divine providence that one particular document was selected and read that night. It was the account of Mordecai's action to expose the two conspirators who were plotting to kill the king.

It was found written that Mordecai had told of Bigthana and Teresh, two of the king's eunuchs, the doorkeepers who had sought to lay hands on King Ahasuerus. Then the king said, "What honor or dignity has been bestowed on Mordecai for this?" And the king's servants who attended him said, "Nothing has been done for him." (Esther 6:2–3)

Mordecai had reported the assassination plot to Queen Esther five years earlier, but he had gone unrewarded. A grateful Ahasuerus was eager to rectify that oversight.

Meanwhile, early the next morning, Haman arrived at the royal court with another deadly request—that the king would authorize the execution of Mordecai. But before Haman could say anything, Ahasuerus posed an open question to him, "What shall be done for the man whom the king delights to honor?" (v. 6). Sure that the king was referring to him and was being so generous as to give him what he thought he should receive, Haman was glad to answer. He eagerly rattled off a grandiose list—including wearing a royal robe, riding on one of the king's horses, and having a prince lead the horse throughout the city while proclaiming, "Thus shall it be done to the man whom the king delights to honor!" Those were honors Haman couldn't wait to enjoy. In a shocking twist of expectations, he heard Ahasuerus say to him:

> Hurry, take the robe and the horse, as you have suggested, and do so for Mordecai the Jew who sits within the king's gate! Leave nothing undone of all that you have spoken. (v. 10)

Filled with humiliation, shame, and rage, Haman had no choice but to do as he was told. So he arrayed Mordecai in splendor and led him throughout the city, making proclamations of praise to him as he went.

Utterly disgraced, Haman hurried home. If he was looking for comfort from his family and friends, he didn't find it. According to verse 13, "When Haman told his wife Zeresh and all his friends everything that had happened to him, his wise men and his wife Zeresh said to him, 'If Mordecai, before whom you have begun to fall, is of Jewish descent, you will not prevail against him but will surely fall before him.'" Their ominous words would soon prove to be prophetic. The tables had been turned. The plot was thickening, and it was pressing in on Haman.

ESTHER PLEADS FOR HER PEOPLE

Later that same day, Haman went back to the palace to attend the second banquet with the king and queen. He undoubtedly tried to steady his heart rate after what had happened that morning, trying to convince himself that somehow he would survive. Haman, however, was in for another horrifying surprise.

The king, overwhelmed by affection for his queen, asked Esther again what it was that she wanted. This time, the queen did not hesitate—poignantly expressing the angst that weighed heavy on her soul. With tears in her eyes and a quiver in her voice, she pleaded,

> If I have found favor in your sight, O king, and if it pleases the king, let my life be given me at my petition, and my people at my request. For we have been sold, my people and I, to be destroyed, to be killed, and to be annihilated. (Esther 7:3–4)

Ahasuerus could not believe what he was hearing. To threaten the queen's life was the height of treason! Instantly incensed, the king demanded to know: "Who is he, and where is he, who would dare presume in his heart to do such a thing?" (v. 5).

As he watched himself becoming the object of the drama, Haman's mind must have been reeling. The noose was tightening around his own neck. Surely the queen was not a Jew, was she? How could he have missed such an important detail? Haman didn't have long to think about his stupendous blunder—only until he heard Esther, with her hand pointed at the red-faced dinner guest, answer Ahasuerus with these words: "The adversary and enemy is this wicked Haman!" (v. 6).

Gorged with fury, the king rose and stormed out into the palace garden. In that moment, he must have remembered the empire-wide pogrom that Haman had convinced him to authorize a couple months earlier. He had been swayed at the time based on Haman's misrepresentation of the Jewish people as a potential threat to the empire. Now the king realized he had been conned into making an unalterable decree that demanded the death of his own queen.

Still inside and at the table, Haman faced his doom. He fell at Esther's feet, in front of the couch where she sat. In desperation, he begged for his life. Ahasuerus, returning from the garden and blinded by anger, interpreted Haman's outstretched plea for mercy as another act of violence against the queen. With a roar of passionate rage, he cried out indignantly, "Will he also assault the queen while I am in the house?" (v. 8). Instantly, royal guards covered Haman's face and led him away to be executed. In an ironic reversal, Haman's body was hanged on the very gallows he had built for Mordecai.

What a difference a day makes! Twenty-four hours earlier, Haman had been at the top of his political career, boasting to family and friends about his royal success and happily plotting the demise of his arch-nemesis, Mordecai, along with all the Jews. That was yesterday. Today, the king would execute him as an enemy of the state. Upon his death, Haman's property became the possession of the king, who gave it to Queen Esther. In turn, she gave it to her cousin Mordecai, placing him in charge of Haman's former estate. The king also exalted him in the royal court (Esther 8:2; 9:4). Esther's risky and courageous action had not only saved Mordecai's life, but also canceled a decree to destroy the Jews.

THE JEWISH PEOPLE ARE SPARED

There was still a hurdle in this cancelation. According to Persian law, the king's edicts could not be reversed (cf. Esther 1:19). But Ahasuerus gladly allowed Esther and Mordecai to issue an official counter-decree, enabling the Jews to defend themselves when their enemies tried to fulfill that decree. Haman's decree had been made two months earlier, giving Esther and her people nearly nine months to prepare their defenses. On top of that, because of Mordecai's exaltation within the Persian government,

> All the officials of the provinces, the satraps, the governors, and all those doing the king's work, helped the Jews, because the fear of Mordecai fell upon them. For Mordecai was great in the king's palace, and his fame spread throughout all the provinces; for this man Mordecai became increasingly prominent. (Esther 9:3–4)

When doomsday finally came—on March 7, 473 BC—the Jews not only defended themselves ably in defeating their enemies throughout the Persian Empire, but in the capital city of Shushan, they killed five hundred ten who opposed them, and another three hundred on the following day. Throughout the empire, an additional seventy-five thousand enemies were slain. The day intended for their destruction became a day of great victory; not only were the Jews not annihilated, as Haman had planned, but their influence throughout the empire actually became stronger. Instead of being a day to remember the extermination of the Jews, it became the day to celebrate their deliverance.

To commemorate that, Mordecai established the feast of Purim—a name derived from the Hebrew word for *lots*. Haman had cast lots to determine the day on which the mass execution of the Jews should occur. Yet in the end, it proved to be a day of triumph and celebration for the Jewish people. Because they continued to vanquish their enemies on the following day, the feast of Purim became a traditional Jewish two-day celebration. Esther 9:23–28 explains,

> So the Jews accepted the custom which they had begun, as Mordecai had written to them, because Haman, the son of Hammedatha the Agagite, the enemy of all the Jews, had plotted against the Jews to annihilate them, and had cast Pur (that is, the lot), to consume them and destroy them; but when Esther came

before the king, he commanded by letter that this wicked plot which Haman had devised against the Jews should return on his own head, and that he and his sons should be hanged on the gallows. So they called these days Purim, after the name Pur. Therefore, because of all the words of this letter, what they had seen concerning this matter, and what had happened to them, the Jews established and imposed it upon themselves and their descendants and all who would join them, that without fail they should celebrate these two days every year, according to the written instructions and according to the prescribed time, that these days should be remembered and kept throughout every generation, every family, every province, and every city, that these days of Purim should not fail to be observed among the Jews, and that the memory of them should not perish among their descendants.

The annual, two-day holiday of feasting, called Purim, has been an event marked by rejoicing, food sharing, gift giving, and memorial fasting (9:21–22, 31). Though it is not mentioned in Scripture outside of Esther, Purim has been celebrated throughout the centuries in Israel and by Jews everywhere—in remembrance of that day long ago when the Jews were providentially rescued from their enemies.

Long after Haman was hanged, Mordecai and Esther continued to flourish in the royal house of King Ahasuerus. The king exalted Mordecai to second-in-command over the entire empire. As Joseph and Daniel had been, Mordecai was elevated to a position of immense power and influence. His experience as an individual—going from the brink of death as a lowly target of hatred to the height of power as a recipient of royal honor—was representative of the experience of Jews throughout the land. Against all odds, Esther, Mordecai, and the Jews had been spared, and not only spared, but elevated. Thus, the book of Esther ends with these hope-filled words:

For Mordecai the Jew was second to King Ahasuerus, and was great among the Jews and well received by the multitude of his brethren, seeking the good of his people and speaking peace to all his countrymen. (Esther 10:3)

WHERE IS GOD IN THE BOOK OF ESTHER?

The real hero in this story is never mentioned, never even named. But every reader knows who He is and sees His heroic acts of power. God Himself is the only explanation for the survival of the Jews in the midst of such hatred and opposition. His hand of providence is in every large event and every small detail as He protects and preserves His people. Song of Solomon and Esther are the only books of the Bible where no reference to God is made. This has understandably caused some readers of Scripture to wonder, Why would the Persian king be referenced over 175 times, while the divine King is not mentioned once?

But His presence comes through more powerfully and more dominantly because it is so obvious that only God could sovereignly ordain everything in the story of Esther. His providence is at work in the fact that, of the twenty-five million women in the Persian Empire, Esther—a Jew—was chosen as the queen; in Mordecai's stumbling upon a plot to assassinate the king and being inadvertently overlooked and unrewarded for it at the time; in that Ahasuerus, on the night he could not sleep, just "happened" to be reading about Mordecai in the royal archives; and in that Haman's timing was perfect—except in the exact opposite way that he intended. In all these and countless other details, the invisible hand of God is unmistakably evident. Even the fact that the feast of Purim was named after the casting of lots reminds us of God's sovereign power over all things: "For the lot is cast into the lap, But its every decision is from the LORD" (Proverbs 16:33). So why is He never mentioned?

The absence is undoubtedly intentional. It is part of a startling yet ingenious literary strategy that actually draws the reader to think deeply about God. The omission is so glaring that the silence screams for our attention and compels us to take notice. There are too many "coincidences" to happen randomly. This amazing narrative calls for a designer, a coordinator—and it is God. By never mentioning His name, the writer has forced us to ask the ultimate question: *Who is doing this?* And in answering that question, one discovers the true hero of the story.

Though it is silent as to His name, God thunders through the book of Esther. The Lord's unseen power is obvious, sovereignly ordaining every detail to preserve His people. There are no miracles in the book, but the remarkable protection of the Jews through God's providential control of every circumstantial detail of people, places, time, and action is nothing short of miraculous—revealing the Lord's infinite wisdom and omnipotence over all things. Coincidence and chance play no role. Even mighty Ahasuerus was under God's sovereign power, evidencing the truth of Proverbs 21:1, "The king's heart is in the hand of the LORD, Like the rivers of water; He turns it wherever He wishes." God superintended the emperor's decisions, even in choosing a new queen. Though His name never appears in the book, He is obviously the dominant actor in the unfolding drama.

The book of Esther might be compared to a chess match, in which God and Satan (working behind the scenes) moved real-life kings, queens, and nobles. It looked as though Satan, using Haman, might put God's plans in check. But the Lord—who has absolute power over Satan—checkmated the devil's schemes by positioning Mordecai and Esther to find favor with the king.

Ever since Adam and Eve fell into sin, Satan has worked to thwart God's plan of salvation. If he had been able to annihilate the Jews in the days of Esther, Satan would have destroyed the messianic line before the Messiah was born, and all the promises to Israel would go unfulfilled. Scripture would be wrong and God dethroned. But God did not let that happen. Even after Jesus came, Satan tried to use Herod (Matthew 2:16), Judas Iscariot (Luke 22:3–6), and even Peter (Matthew 16:22) to derail Christ's earthly mission. Yet on every occasion, the purposes of God prevailed, just as they did in Esther. His name might not be mentioned in the book, but God's handiwork is clearly evident on every page. Time after time, He overturned Satan's malevolent schemes through His providential intervention.

Queen Esther, along with Mordecai, were the human instruments God used to rescue His covenant people from total destruction. Esther, who came from humble beginnings, was an orphan in a foreign land hundreds of miles from Israel. As such, she truly was an unlikely hero. The Lord's plans for her were astounding and unimaginable, as He placed her in a position of prominence to protect the Jews from evil intentions.

Through Haman, Satan attempted to put the Abrahamic and Davidic promises to Israel in jeopardy (cf. Genesis 17:1–8; 2 Samuel 7:8–16). But against the dark backdrop of heinous evil, both God's covenant love for Israel and His power to protect them shone brightly in spectacular ways. Today, as the drama of world events continues to unfold, and evil powers in the Middle East threaten the existence of Israel again (just as European powers did in the days of Hitler and Stalin), the Lord will preserve the Jews for final salvation in the future; the kingdom He has promised to them through His prophets will come. As the apostle Paul explained in Romans 11:26–29:

> And so all Israel will be saved, as it is written:
> "The Deliverer will come out of Zion,
> And He will turn away ungodliness from Jacob;
> For this is My covenant with them,
> When I take away their sins."
> . . . For the gifts and the calling of God are irrevocable.

The Lord is still on the throne of the universe, just as He was in Esther's day. He is absolutely sovereign over the governments and earthly rulers of the modern era. Though the news reports rarely mention His name, God is the unseen power behind it all, perfectly orchestrating the details to accomplish His purposes. In the words of Psalm 103:19, "The Lord has established His throne in heaven, and His kingdom rules over all." What a comfort that is to all those who have put their trust in Him!

8

JOHN THE BAPTIST: THE TRUE MEANING OF GREATNESS

———⊤———

As they departed, Jesus began to say to the multitudes concerning John: "What did you go out into the wilderness to see? . . . A prophet? Yes, I say to you, and more than a prophet. For this is he of whom it is written: 'Behold, I send My messenger before Your face, who will prepare Your way before You.' Assuredly, I say to you, among those born of women there has not risen one greater than John the Baptist."

—MATTHEW 11:7–11

WHAT DOES GOD MEAN when He designates someone as great? In the thinking of popular culture, greatness is usually defined in terms of privilege, accomplishment, money, and power leading to some means of fame. A truer view of greatness, albeit less popular, centers on someone's lasting significance for providing far-reaching benefits to people, not just personal celebrity status; it elevates those who impact the world in significant and positive ways. But whether we measure greatness from the standpoint of popularity or from the standpoint of human achievement, both definitions fall woefully short of God's perspective.

Using either of those criteria for greatness, John the Baptist would not be deemed great. He was not born into a wealthy or powerful family. His parents, Zacharias and Elizabeth, were both from the priestly tribe of Levi. But there were many Levites in Israel at the time—so many that John's family did not have any special social status. While still a teenager, John abandoned the comforts and conveniences of civilized society and moved out into the Judean wilderness, becoming a hermit-like, homeless, wilderness preacher. According to Matthew 3:4, "John himself was clothed in camel's hair, with a leather belt around his waist; and his food was locusts and wild honey." Nothing about his lineage, his contrary social behavior, his external appearance, or his diet suggested that he should be considered anything but odd.

He was cut off from formal education, living in isolation in the desert. Though he came from a priestly line, he wasn't associated with the priesthood. He was linked to neither wealth nor royalty. He instigated no permanent social, political, or religious movement. Though the populace was drawn to his message of the Messiah's arrival, the authorities (such as the Pharisees and scribes) resented him fiercely. In turn, he rebuked them and warned them of divine judgment, like a brood of snakes caught in a raging brushfire. Only a small band of disciples continued to follow him briefly. His ministry was relatively short; he died ignominiously at the hands of a petty ruler named Herod who was seduced by a lewd young girl's dance. When Herod told her he would give her anything she wanted, she commiserated with her mother, Herod's wife, who wanted her to ask for John's head on a silver platter. Nothing in his life fit the model associated with greatness.

In spite of all that, he was what the angel Gabriel said he would be: "great in the sight of the Lord" (Luke 1:15). Incredibly, the Lord not only declared him to be a great man, but the *greatest* man who had ever lived. That declaration came from the lips of Jesus Christ Himself: "Assuredly, I say to you, among those born of women there has not risen one greater than John the Baptist" (Matthew 11:11). "Born of women" was a common expression referring to humanness in general. Thus, Jesus was saying, in essence, "No greater human being has ever lived."

In our examination of God's unlikely heroes, we have already looked at some of the Bible's most compelling characters. Yet the Messiah Himself declared that John the Baptist was greater than any other Old Testament saint! He was greater than Enoch, Abraham, Moses, Samson, David, or any of the prophets. He was greater than all those listed in Hebrews 11 as the monumental heroes of the faith. No king, military commander, or philosopher was greater than John. He was the greatest person who had ever lived up to that time, both in terms of task and privilege.

That was clear from the start of his story.

BREAKING THE SILENCE

Before John the Baptist, there had been no prophet in Israel for over four centuries. Since the days of Malachi, no new word of revelation had come from heaven. Nor had an angel appeared to men since the time of the prophet Zechariah, five hundred years earlier. But that long silence was about to be broken.

The year was approximately 5 BC, and the setting Jerusalem. An elderly and ordinary priest named Zacharias (named in honor of the Old Testament prophet) was brimming with anticipation as he approached the holy place of the temple. Once inside, he would be privileged to offer burnt incense on the sacred altar. This event would mark the high point of his priestly career, and Zacharias must have wanted to relish every moment. But even his most elevated expectations could not have prepared him for what he was to experience.

Zacharias was a priest in the order of Abijah, one of the twenty-four orders of the Jewish priesthood named for the grandsons of

Aaron. Each priestly order was responsible to serve two separate weeks per year at the temple in Jerusalem. When the time came, the priests in the order of Abijah, including Zacharias, traveled to Israel's capital city to fulfill their sacred duties.

Priestly responsibilities included one of the priests offering incense every morning and every evening inside the temple's holy place (cf. Exodus 30:7–8). As that lone priest made his way to the altar of incense, the rest of the order, along with all the people, were to stand outside and pray. The incense would arise from the altar as a sweet-smelling symbol of the prayers of the nation to God.

Because there were many priests but only one could offer incense each morning and each evening, most would never participate in that sacred task. The privileged priest was selected by the casting of lots, and once chosen, he could never be chosen again. So to offer incense in the holy place was a once-in-a-lifetime experience. When elderly Zacharias was selected, after decades of faithful service, he would have been barely able to contain his excitement.

Without question, this was the pinnacle of his priestly life. The altar of incense was just outside the veil that separated the holy place from the Holy of Holies, meaning that it was as close to the presence of God as any priest could ever go. No common person was allowed in the holy place, and only the high priest could go farther into the Holy of Holies, and that was only once a year.

As eager and fulfilled as Zacharias was when he entered the holy place, he had no intention to stay too long. Conforming to the pre-scribed ceremony, he carried a small bowl full of the burning coals from off the brazen altar, the altar of burnt offering. Making his way to the altar of incense, he poured the coals in and spread them around. Then he covered them with the incense so that a great cloud of sweet-smelling aroma arose from the altar.

Everything was ordinary and routine until the extraordinary occurred and Zacharias was no longer alone. Suddenly, an angel from heaven appeared and stood with him next to the altar. The startled priest was shocked and terrified. In the understated words of Luke 1:12, "When Zacharias saw him, he was troubled, and fear fell upon him." Zacharias was nearly scared to death. There he was, in the holy place—closer to the presence of almighty God than he had ever been in his life, knowing that other priests in Israel's history had been judged for offering unacceptable incense before the Lord (cf. Leviticus 10:1–2). Instantly, Zacharias must have wondered if he had done something to displease God and the angel was there to announce his judgment. But that was not the case.

The angel Gabriel was there to bring the most wondrous news anyone could ever have heard at that time—news concerning the arrival of the Messiah. It started with these words: "Do not be afraid, Zacharias, for your prayer is heard; and your wife Elizabeth will bear you a son, and you shall call his name John" (Luke 1:13).

The reality of just that promise was nearly as astonishing as the angel's sudden appearance had been. Zacharias and his wife Elizabeth were old—at least in their sixties and maybe in their seventies or eighties. They were painfully childless, and Elizabeth was far past the age for getting pregnant. But God would do for Elizabeth what He had done ages before for Sarah and Hannah, open her womb and give her a son. Barrenness, a reproach in ancient Israel, was about to be supernaturally removed. The long-empty womb would miraculously hold a son. And the name *John*, which means "God is gracious," would always remind them of the special favor God had bestowed upon them.

As he struggled to recover from his initial shock, Zacharias could not believe what the angel was saying. But Gabriel's incredible message was not finished. Not only would his wife bear a son through supernatural circumstances, but that son would become in many ways the most exceptional prophet ever. As the angel explained to the astonished priest:

And you will have joy and gladness, and many will rejoice at his birth. For he will be great in the sight of the Lord, and shall drink neither wine nor strong drink. He will also be filled with the Holy Spirit, even from his mother's womb. And he will turn many of the children of Israel to the Lord their God. He will also go before Him in the spirit and power of Elijah, "to turn the hearts of the fathers to the children," and the disobedient to the wisdom of the just, to make ready a people prepared for the Lord. (Luke 1:14–17)

After four hundred silent years, this prophet would announce the arrival of the Messiah. Zacharias's son was to be the Messiah's herald!

This news was so unbelievable that Zacharias did not believe it. In response to his doubt and the subsequent doubts of everyone he would tell about the angel's words, Gabriel gave him a sign: "Behold, you will be mute and not able to speak until the day these things take place, because you did not believe my words which will be fulfilled in their own time" (Luke 1:20). Having used his voice to express sinful doubt, Zacharias would be unable to use again it until his son was born. But in a backward way that silence would be verification of the supernatural encounter.

That became apparent when he finally emerged from the Holy Place and was greeted with the bewildered stares and queries of the Jewish congregation gathered at the temple. What had taken him so long? And why did he have such a dumbfounded look on his face? To the crowd's further surprise, Zacharias was unable to offer any audible explanation for his delay. Finally, after deciphering his hand motions, "they perceived that he had seen a vision in the temple, for he beckoned to them and remained speechless" (v. 22). His frustrated silence was evidence of a divine revelation.

As he finished up his responsibilities in Jerusalem and headed back home to Elizabeth, Zacharias's mind must have rambled through all the potential scenarios. A short time later, his elderly wife conceived; and nine months after that, baby John was born. But even before he was born, the baby was filled with the Holy Spirit (v. 15), such that he was bouncing in Elizabeth's womb when her cousin Mary, the mother of Jesus, came for a visit (v. 41).

Zacharias didn't speak a word until after John's birth. For almost a year, he had knowledge of the greatest news ever and couldn't speak it. When his baby boy was brought to be circumcised, his tongue was instantly loose. He must have gushed out the full magnitude of what he had been thinking about during all those months. After praising the Lord for His covenant faithfulness to Israel, the proud father blessed his eight-day old son with inspired words:

> *And you, child, will be called the prophet of the Highest;*
> *For you will go before the face of the Lord to prepare His ways,*
> *To give knowledge of salvation to His people*
> *By the remission of their sins,*
> *Through the tender mercy of our God,*
> *With which the Dayspring from on high has visited us;*
> *To give light to those who sit in darkness and the shadow of death,*
> *To guide our feet into the way of peace.* (Luke 1:76–79)

Those powerful words would come to characterize the radical ministry of this extraordinary prophet.

A VOICE CRYING IN THE WILDERNESS

After recounting his incredible birth, the biblical record quickly moves forward to the beginnings of John's ministry. He lived much of his life in the obscurity of the Judean desert before the word of God came to him initiating his prophetic ministry when he was about thirty years old (Luke 3:2). At that time, he suddenly "came baptizing in the wilderness and preaching a baptism of repentance for the remission of sins" (Mark 1:4).

John was a contrast in every respect—from his prolonged isolation to his abrupt public appearance, from his rugged wilderness life to his dramatic preaching and baptizing ministry. He was born to a woman who could not have children. He came from a line of priests, but ministered as a prophet. And he reached Jewish society by removing himself from it.

Both his training and his ministry took place in the unpopulated desert. That might seem like an odd place for the forerunner of the Messiah to set up his headquarters. But it fit perfectly with God's plan. John was not sent to the royal courts of the ancient world to announce the coming of the King of the universe. From an obscure family, with a strange lifestyle, he established his ministry squarely in the middle of nowhere.

But all of that was purposeful, a radical approach intended to awaken the people from their spiritual slumber and call them out of the dead legalism of their religious practices. Constantly flowing crowds from Jerusalem and Jericho, driven by both curiosity and conviction, came out to hear the eccentric prophet preach. There in the desolate sands, removed from the distractions of the city and the oppression of the religious leaders, people were able to carefully ponder the powerful truths John was proclaiming.

John's message was as startling as his physical appearance. He claimed to be the true messenger from God, but was not like the well-mannered, soft-spoken, and richly adorned Pharisees and Sadducees. John's scratchy camel's hair cloak, plain leather belt, and diet of locusts and wild honey served as a metaphoric and stinging rebuke to the leaders of Israel's religious establishment. Like the Old Testament prophets before him, everything about John's strange behavior was intended as an object lesson for God's chosen nation. He was not calling others to live or dress as he did, but he was calling people away from liturgically dressed hypocrites who were leading people to hell.

THE KINGDOM IS AT HAND

As the preacher privileged to announce the arrival of the Messiah, John's calling was more lofty and sacred than that of anyone who had come before him. His was the first prophetic voice to echo throughout the Judean hillsides since the prophet Malachi went silent four hundred years earlier. Though his story is told in the Gospels, John was the last of the Old Testament prophets. As such, he was given the privileged responsibility of both announcing the Messiah's coming and declaring His arrival. Like his predecessors, John faithfully pointed people forward to Christ, but unlike the other Jewish prophets, he lived to see the fulfillment of his words.

In Matthew 11:9, Jesus separated John from the noble prophets before him by saying he was "more than a prophet" because—as the Lord went on to explain—he was the divinely appointed messenger foretold in Malachi 3:1. John's mission had been prophesied some seven hundred years earlier by Isaiah: "The voice of one crying in the wilderness: 'Prepare the way of the LORD; Make His paths straight'" (Matthew 3:3; cf. Isaiah 40:3–4). He was preparing the hearts of the Jews for the coming of their long-awaited King. After millennia of anticipation and prophetic promises, John was selected for the unparalleled privilege of being the Messiah's personal herald.

In the ancient near east, the coming of a monarch was usually preceded by the appearance of a herald who announced the king's imminent arrival and made final preparations for his stay. Along with the herald, a delegation of servants would be sent ahead of the royal caravan in order to remove any obstacles in the road and make sure the way was ready for travel. Thus the herald's responsibility was two-fold: to proclaim the king's coming and to prepare the way for his arrival. Those two components defined the privileged ministry of John the Baptist.

But John did not serve merely a human king. He was the fore-runner of the King of kings. As such, he did not clear debris from literal roads; rather, through his Spirit-empowered preaching on repentance and faith, he sought to remove the obstacles of un-belief from the hearts of sinful men and women. He challenged the hypocritical self-righteousness of first-century Judaism and called people to repent and live a life of holy faith and obedience. In this way, they would be prepared for the coming of the Messiah and His kingdom.

John's ministry is described as "the voice of one crying in the wilderness." To all who would listen, his thundering words reiterated one simple message: "Repent!" (Matthew 3:2). The Greek word for *repent* entails more than mere sorrow or regret. It means "to change the mind and will" and encompasses the idea of turning around and heading in the opposite direction. Repentance does not refer to just any change, but to a change from sin to righteousness. It involves sorrow over sin, but goes beyond that to produce both changed thinking and the desire for a changed life (cf. 2 Corinthians 7:10). John declared that if the people would turn from their rebellious pride and embrace a life of wholehearted obedience, they would be ready for the Messiah.

John's message shocked the Jewish people, who assumed they were already included because they belonged to God's chosen nation. By ethnicity, they felt assured of a place in the kingdom of heaven, such that repentance was not necessary for them. On the other hand, the neighboring Gentile nations had no such privilege. John con-fronted that false notion head on, boldly declaring, "Do not think to say to yourselves, 'We have Abraham as our father.' For I say to you that God is able to raise up children to Abraham from these stones" (Matthew 3:9). To the self-righteous Israelites who heard, John's point was unmistakably clear: they were in the exact same condition as the unbelieving Gentiles—spiritually dead, like stones. Unless they repented and were converted from sin to righteousness, they would not inherit eternal salvation. Instead, they would be judged. Being Jewish—and religious, at that—counted for nothing before God but greater judgment.

John's mandate was urgent. The coming of the King was imminent. In spite of their religion, the people's hearts were hard and cold. So John confronted them with fiery passion and unabashed directness. Now was not the time to mince words. He challenged the people to turn away from the ritualism, superficiality, and hypocrisy of their external ceremonies, traditions, and laws. He called them away from the establishment, into the wilderness, to a place where they would not have gone unless they were serious about repenting. He exposed the false pretenses of the religious leaders with vivid warnings, and he challenged the people to demonstrate their repentance in practical ways, like caring for the needy, working with integrity, and showing love to others (Luke 3:11–14).

He preached with such conviction and authority that some who heard him thought he might actually be the Messiah himself. But John quickly dismissed such misguided rumors. When questioned by the priests and Levites who had been sent from Jerusalem to ask his identity, John replied, "I am not the Christ" (John 1:19–20). He likewise told the crowds, "I indeed baptize you with water; but One mightier than I is coming, whose sandal strap I am not worthy to loose. He will baptize you with the Holy Spirit and fire" (Luke 3:16).

John knew his position and his task. Thus he never sought honor for himself, but only for the One whose coming he proclaimed. From childhood, John had undoubtedly been told many times of the angel's announcement of his birth and his calling—a purpose he never compromised or manipulated for his own gain.

Though he ministered out in the wilderness, John's preaching had a dramatic impact in the cities of Israel. According to Matthew's account, "Then Jerusalem, all Judea, and all the region around the Jordan went out to him and were baptized by him in the Jordan, confessing their sins" (3:5–6). Multitudes traveled to hear him preach, and many were convicted of their sin and baptized as a symbol of their desire for repentance and readiness to receive the Messiah.

Unlike Levitical ceremonial washings, which involved repeatedly washing the hands, feet, and head to symbolize the need for continual purification from recurring sin, the baptism of John was a onetime event. The closest parallel, in the Jewish practices of that day, was a ritual not intended for native Israelites at all—the baptism of Gentile proselytes upon their entrance into Judaism.

That parallel would not have been lost on the Jews to whom John preached. Those who were truly repentant needed to recognize that rather than being superior, they were no better than pagan non-Jews, spiritually speaking. Even though they were Abraham's physical descendants, until they repented, they were complete outsiders to God's kingdom. In order to symbolize their recognition of that reality, John called the Jews to be baptized in the same way as a Gentile proselyte.

BAPTIZING THE KING

The exact location of John's baptizing ministry along the Jordan River is unknown. The apostle John notes that it was near "Bethabara [or Bethany] beyond the Jordan" (1:28), but archeologists are uncertain as to the precise location of that ancient town. It was likely toward the southern end of the river, near Jericho and the Dead Sea—which is why the inhabitants who flocked to hear John preach were from nearby Jerusalem and Jericho.

John may have been surprised when the huge crowds came to hear him, especially when the antagonistic scribes and Pharisees showed up. But he was absolutely shocked when Jesus, the King Himself, appeared in the crowd and asked to be baptized. Surely, if anyone did *not* need a baptism of repentance, it was the Messiah, the sinless Son of God! Accordingly, Matthew 3:14–15 says,

John tried to prevent Him, saying, "I need to be baptized by You, and are You coming to me?" But Jesus answered and said to him, "Permit it to be so now, for thus it is fitting for us to fulfill all righteousness." Then he allowed Him.

As unthinkable as it was, Jesus had purposefully come to John to be baptized. When he first saw Jesus coming toward him, John declared, "Behold! The Lamb of God who takes away the sin of the world! This is He of whom I said, 'After me comes a Man who is preferred before me, for He was before me'" (John 1:29–30). In that brief salutation, the baptizing prophet expressed the profound truth of Jesus' Person and mission—noting both Christ's redemptive work as the Lamb of God and His eternality as the Son of God. Understandably, John's first reaction was that the Redeemer ought to baptize him, not the other way around.

John's baptism was a way for sinners to physically symbolize their repentance from sin. But Jesus came to be baptized even though He was absolutely sinless. Bewildered, John must have wondered, "Why would the perfect One who takes away the sins of the world want to participate in a ceremony that symbolizes a turning from sin?"

Jesus patiently explained to John that although it might seem confusing, He must be baptized in order to "fulfill all righteousness." What did He mean by that? Simply that John's baptism was from God who ordained it as an act of righteousness, required by God. And Jesus did all things that God declared to be righteous as part of His total obedience to His Father.

The baptism of Jesus also demonstrated three other related things. First, it portrayed His willingness to identify with the sinners whom He came to save. As the first act of His public ministry, the Friend of Sinners associated Himself with those who were unrighteous—by submitting to a baptism designed for sinners. Second, His baptism served as a symbol of His death and resurrection. It prefigured the final act of His public ministry, His crucifixion and subsequent victory over death. Finally, Jesus' baptism served as a coronation ceremony and as a fitting beginning to His public work. When He came out of the water, God the Father commissioned Him with a voice from heaven. In the words of Matthew,

> When He had been baptized, Jesus came up immediately from the water; and behold, the heavens were opened to Him, and He saw the Spirit of God descending like a dove and alighting upon Him. And suddenly a voice came from heaven, saying, "This is My beloved Son, in whom I am well pleased." (Matthew 3:16–17)

For Jesus, His baptism marked the beginning of His preaching ministry. For John, it was the climax of his God-given task. The faithful forerunner had fulfilled his mission to proclaim Christ's coming and prepare the way for His arrival.

After this point, John intentionally sought a diminishing role as he continued to point people away from himself and toward Jesus Christ. He encouraged his disciples to become followers of Jesus (John 1:34–36), and when some of his other disciples became jealous of Jesus' popularity, John told them:

> You yourselves bear me witness, that I said, "I am not the Christ," but, "I have been sent before Him." He who has the bride is the bridegroom; but the friend of the bridegroom, who stands and hears him, rejoices greatly because of the bridegroom's voice. Therefore this joy of mine is fulfilled. He must increase, but I must decrease. (John 3:28–30).

With no desire to compete with Christ, John joyously deferred to Him. His calling had been accomplished, and John moved into the background, then prison and death.

JOHN'S FINAL DAYS

From an earthly perspective, John's life and career ended in disaster. He had been a zealous, fearless prophet, faithfully fulfilling his role and boldly saying exactly what God called him to say. He was courageous and confrontational, but his unwavering commitment to the Lord landed him in prison.

Here's how.

While on a visit to Rome, Herod Antipas, who governed Galilee for the Romans, seduced a married woman named Herodias. To make it even uglier, she was from his own family—the wife of his brother Philip. When he returned to Galilee, Herod divorced his own wife and married Herodias, thereby committing both adultery and incest. John the Baptist, as a confrontational preacher against sin, openly exposed Herod's gross immorality. Herod retaliated by having John promptly arrested and thrown into prison. If it were not for John's popularity with the people, which Herod feared, the wicked ruler would have killed him immediately (Matthew 14:5).

The rugged prophet was taken to an old fort in Machaerus, located in a desolate desert region near the Dead Sea. Trading the freedom of open wilderness for a small pit, he suffered long months of shame, physical torment, and loneliness. When he would hear reports about Jesus, they bewildered him. Like all the Jews at that time, John expected the Messiah to establish the earthly kingdom of righteousness and peace the prophets had promised. (Though Christ *will* set up His millennial kingdom at His return, that was not the purpose of His first coming.) Instead, Jesus was carrying on a ministry of healing, not judgment; and He was headquartered in Galilee, far from Jerusalem, the city of the King. He was with the outcasts and common people and hated by the leaders. John wondered if he had misunderstood Jesus' agenda. And so, after about a year, John sent two of his disciples to Jesus to ask Him, "Are You the Coming One, or do we look for another?" (Matthew 11:3).

Without question, John was a true believer in the Lord Jesus and a loyal prophet of God who had proven himself faithful. When baptizing Jesus, John had heard God the Father audibly declare Jesus to be His beloved Son and witnessed the Holy Spirit descending upon Him. Even while in prison, he had heard about Jesus' miraculous powers. Yet, perhaps questioning the dire circumstances that he continued to endure and wondering why Jesus had not yet established His rule, John became confused.

But John knew right where to go for answers to his questions. He sent his disciples to Jesus for clarity and assurance that He was the Christ. With compassion and kindness, Jesus gladly responded to John, saying to John's disciples:

> Go and tell John the things which you hear and see: The blind see and the lame walk; the lepers are cleansed and the deaf hear; the dead are raised up and the poor have the gospel preached to them. And blessed is he who is not offended because of Me. (Matthew 11:4–6)

Jesus' words were no rebuke, but rather a loving confirmation of His true identity. Seemingly, Christ performed these miracles in the presence of John's disciples so that they could report back that they had personally seen proof that He was indeed the Messiah. That was the hope John wanted confirmed, even if the plan for Christ's kingdom was different from what John had expected.

John's disciples took the news of what they had witnessed back to the incarcerated prophet. Though the Scriptures don't tell us what happened, the implication is that Jesus' message had its intended effect. John's questions were answered and his concerns laid to rest.

Though John's circumstances did not change and he was soon executed, Jesus' response was enough to encourage him and renew his faith and confidence. After John was beheaded by Herod, "his disciples came and took away the body and buried it, and went and told Jesus" (Matthew 14:12). They went to Jesus because they knew He would want to know about the death of the greatest prophet ever and His own faithful herald.

A GREATNESS LIKE JOHN'S

Of all the heroes in Israel's history, John the Baptist, though the greatest, was also one of the most unlikely. We've already noted some of the characteristics that made him unique: his extraordinary birth, wilderness upbringing, eccentric clothing, exotic diet, fiery preaching, and ministry of baptism. John possessed none of the qualities society usually associates with greatness. He was not like any of the religious or political leaders of his day. Yet God chose him to fulfill the highest privilege of any religious person who had ever lived. Throughout his life, John exhibited genuine humility, passionate devotion to God's revelation, and a Christ-centered focus. For those reasons, he is rightly considered a great hero of the faith.

From the world's point of view, he achieved nothing of lasting value. Rather, he was hated, despised, and decapitated by his enemies. But in terms of divine approval and privilege, no one had ever been given a more noble calling than John. Like many of the other heroes of the faith, John's loyal service to God ultimately cost him his life. The book of Hebrews reports that many of the Old Testament prophets were

. . . tortured, not accepting deliverance, that they might obtain a better resurrection. Still others had trial of mockings and scourgings, yes, and of chains and imprisonment. They were stoned, they were sawn in two, were tempted, were slain with the sword. They wandered about in sheepskins and goatskins, being destitute, afflicted, tormented—of whom the world was not worthy. They wandered in deserts and mountains, in dens and caves of the earth. (Hebrews 11:35–38)

As the last and greatest of the Old Testament prophets, John's ministry similarly ended in martyrdom. Yet, the legacy of his faithfulness shines as brightly as all those who came before him, and it reminds us how true greatness is measured.

It may be a shock to our superficial society to learn that greatness is not defined in terms of human achievement, athletic prowess, financial gain, political power, or celebrity status. Instead, it is measured by how one relates to the person and work of Jesus Christ. John the Baptist was great because of his proximity to the Messiah. Similarly for us, true greatness is found in faithfully acknowledging the Savior. It is derived from our relationship to the One far greater than John—the Lord Jesus Christ.

In Matthew 11:11, after noting the unique greatness of John the Baptist, Jesus went on to make a vivid spiritual point. The Lord explained that "he who is least in the kingdom of heaven is greater than [John]." In saying that, Jesus was not diminishing John's stature; rather, He was emphasizing the spiritual privilege that all New Testament believers enjoy. John was greater than the Old Testament prophets because he personally participated in the fulfillment of what they had merely anticipated from a distance (cf. 1 Peter 1:10–11). But all believers after the cross and resurrection enjoy even greater privilege still because we participate in the full understanding and experience of something John only anticipated—the actual atoning work of Christ.

Upon arriving in heaven, our privilege will be elevated infinitely, as was John's. There, our faith will be sight and our hope will be realized as we praise our Savior face to face. John's unique greatness was with regard to his role in human history. In terms of spiritual inheritance, however, even John's earthly greatness cannot compare to what he and every believer will enjoy in the glories of heaven.

One day we will meet John and for all eternity join with him in worshipping the very Savior whose coming he so faithfully proclaimed: Jesus Christ, the Lamb of God, who takes away the sins of the world.

9

James: The Brother
of Our Lord

Then after three years I went up to Jerusalem to see Peter, and remained
with him fifteen days. But I saw none of the other apostles except James,
the Lord's brother.

—Galatians 1:18–19

W HAT WOULD IT HAVE BEEN LIKE to live and grow
up in the same family as Jesus? For His brothers and
sisters, that question was not hypothetical. It was their
daily reality.

In spite of the traditional claims made by the Roman Catholic
Church, Mary was anything but a perpetual virgin (Matthew 1:25).
After giving birth to Jesus while a virgin, she had a normal sexual
relationship with Joseph that led to her giving birth to at least six
more children. Luke 2:7 implies that she had other children by calling Jesus Mary's *firstborn* son. And Matthew 13:55–56 and Mark
6:3 even list the names of Jesus' brothers: James, Joses, Simon, and
Jude. Those passages also note that Jesus had multiple sisters, though
their names are not given. Jewish families in the first century were

typically large, and the family of Joseph and Mary was no exception. Though Jesus is the only begotten Son of God (John 3:16), He was not the only begotten son of Mary. Seven or more children—five boys (including Jesus) and at least two girls—lived in the house of Joseph and Mary for all their young lives.

Jesus, of course, was not Joseph's biological son. So His siblings were technically His half-brothers and half-sisters. But clearly, because He lived with the family as the earthly son of both Mary and Joseph (Matthew 13:55; Luke 2:48), and as the older brother of His siblings, He was one of them. It was in that context that our Lord developed from boyhood into manhood. For roughly thirty years, He humbly worked as the son of a carpenter in the small village of Nazareth alongside His siblings.

GROWING UP WITH JESUS

So what was it like to grow up in the same household as the divine Son of God?

Through the centuries, that question has inspired countless legends and apocryphal accounts about Jesus' childhood. Mythical stories abound about how as a boy He miraculously purified water, brought clay sparrows to life, resurrected a dead playmate, healed a woodcutter's injured foot, gathered one hundred bushels of wheat from a single grain, lengthened a wooden board for use in Joseph's carpentry shop, raised one of his teachers from the dead, and healed James of a poisonous snake bite. In one account, the young Jesus is worshipped by lions and leopards; in another, He commands a tree to bend down its branches in order to make its fruit easier to pick. According to such legends (and other bizarre superstitions), Jesus regularly employed miracles to make growing up in lowly, pedestrian Nazareth a little more exciting.

But that is not at all how the Bible depicts our Lord's childhood.

Growing up, Jesus appeared in every way to be like any other child. Luke 2:40 summarizes His physical and mental development in these words: "And the Child grew and became strong in spirit, filled with wisdom; and the grace of God was upon Him." With each passing year, His body and mind continued to develop so that He became increasingly capable of understanding and doing more. He actually developed as any child does.

According to Hebrews 5:8, Jesus "learned obedience by the things which He suffered," and Hebrews 4:15 explains that He "was in all points [throughout His life] tempted as we are, yet without sin." Even as a child, He suffered the constant temptations that come at children living in a fallen world—what the apostle John called "the lust of the flesh, the lust of the eyes, and the pride of life" (1 John 2:16). As He grew into "all points," the temptations came that were common to each age and connected to His maturing. The difference between Jesus and others was not in normal development and its temptations. Those He faced like everyone (making Him a merciful and faithful High Priest who has been tempted with all the feelings of our weaknesses); the difference was that He was completely sinless! Like no one who has ever or will ever live, He never had a bad attitude, never disobeyed His parents, never complained about dinner, never bickered with His siblings, never lied, never entertained an evil thought, never gossiped about a friend or slandered an enemy, and never wasted a moment of time. And that was true of Him in every situation and form of temptation for His entire life. It was actually through those temptations, over which He always triumphed, that He learned experientially what it was to obey His heavenly Father in everything all the time. Certainly, this absolute holy perfection made Him both the favorite of His parents and the envy of His siblings. The fact that even His life-long perfection didn't persuade His brothers of His Messiahship (cf. John 7:5) is evidence that they not only envied Him but resented Him.

The only actual, historical glimpse we have into Jesus' childhood comes from Luke 2:40–52, which describes His visit to the temple at age twelve. As they did every year, Mary and Joseph went to Jerusalem to celebrate the Passover, taking Jesus and likely their entire family with them. They traveled with a large caravan of other pilgrims from Nazareth and Galilee, making the four-day journey southeast around Samaria and west up to Jerusalem from Jericho.

After the Passover celebration ended, Joseph and Mary joined the caravan and began the return trip to Nazareth. Never having had reason to question Jesus' reliability and responsibility, they simply assumed He was somewhere in the crowd, probably walking ahead of them with friends or relatives.

Since Jesus was the one child they never had to worry about, it was the end of the first day's journey before they missed Him. Mary and Joseph soon discovered that He had been left behind in Jerusalem. Luke reports:

> When they did not find Him, they returned to Jerusalem, seeking Him. Now so it was that after three days they found Him in the temple, sitting in the midst of the teachers, both listening to them and asking them questions. And all who heard Him were astonished at His understanding and answers. So when they saw Him, they were amazed; and His mother said to Him, "Son, why have You done this to us? Look, Your father and I have sought You anxiously." And He said to them, "Why did you seek Me? Did you not know that I must be about My Father's business?" But they did not understand the statement which He spoke to them. (Luke 2:45–50)

As this dramatic scene demonstrates, by the time Jesus was twelve years old, He had come to a full grasp of exactly who He was and why God had sent Him from heaven to earth. His answer to Mary and Joseph, not at all intended as disrespect toward them, was rather a profound declaration that He knew His identity and His mission.

By calling the great, sacred temple of God the house of His Father, Jesus identified Himself as the Son of God. This was a shocking claim that the Jews saw as blasphemy (cf. John 5:18). But His parents knew it was the truth. Though nothing supernatural happened in that interchange, it was as profoundly divine as a massive miracle.

But even after that monumental declaration, Jesus returned submissively with Mary and Joseph to the family, to live there another eighteen years. According to Luke 2:51, He continued to be subject to them, and in the eyes of his friends and relatives, He resumed regular life. The normalcy of Jesus' childhood and early adulthood is confirmed by the fact that when He began His public ministry, His former neighbors in Nazareth did not believe Him to be the Messiah or the Son of God. Their familiarity with Him produced disdain in their hearts. "Is this not the carpenter's son?" they asked. "Is not His mother called Mary? And His brothers James, Joses, Simon, and Judas [Jude]? And His sisters, are they not all with us? Where then did this Man get all these things?" (Matthew 13:55–56). Because they had always assumed that He was a man like other men, even if more righteous, they refused to believe that He was, in actuality, the redeemer of Israel and the world.

Jesus' brothers were so set in their unbelief that as they watched His ministry, they concluded that the explanation for His outrageous claims was that He was "out of His mind" (Mark 3:21; cf. John 7:5). Their unbelief was inexcusable. It demonstrated the truth of Jesus' declaration that "a prophet is not without honor except in his own country, among his own relatives, and in his own house" (Mark 6:4). But on the other hand, their skepticism bore testimony to the true humanity of Jesus. Clearly, He had not performed any miracles for them while growing up. His miracle working did not commence until the start of His public ministry, which is why John 2:11 states emphatically that the turning of water into wine was "the beginning of signs" that Jesus did.

In the face of all that, the Lord's perfect life stood out as truly and mysteriously extraordinary—a dramatically sharp contrast to the behavior of James, Joses, Simon, Jude, and their sisters. That such vivid testimony did not convict their hearts and convince them of His true identity is evidence that "familiarity breeds contempt" and perfection generates rejection. Incredibly, the glory of God in Jesus produced jealousy in their minds; attitudes that turned to scorn and disdain when Jesus began His public ministry. Throughout history, many younger siblings have resented the high standard of expectation set by the oldest child. But imagine a perfect older brother who never sinned! For the younger brothers of Jesus, their own sinful deficiencies were openly exaggerated by comparison to Him. Like all children, they were disobedient and fell into trouble (and were disciplined as a result), but Jesus never misbehaved. And they were likely hearing from their parents, especially Mary, about how they should follow the example of their older brother. There was plenty of opportunity for seeds of resentment and envy to be planted in their hearts.

Both times that Jesus' brothers are listed in the gospels, James is mentioned first, suggesting that he was the oldest—likely just a year or two younger than Jesus. As the second-born, James had lived with and felt the differences between himself and Jesus longer than his other siblings. After Jesus left Nazareth and began His public ministry, James became the leader of the family. (It is probable, since he is never mentioned, that Joseph had died by that time. At the cross, for example, Mary was clearly a widow—cf. John 19:26–27.) If so, James would have been the spokesman for Jesus' brothers—the one most active in voicing an attitude of criticism and unbelief (cf. John 7:3–5).

THE BELIEVING BROTHER

No indication is given in any of the four gospels that Jesus' brothers came to believe in Him during the years of His public ministry. But after His death, resurrection, and ascension, there is a dramatic and miraculous change. His brothers are present among the believers who have gathered in the upper room, awaiting the coming of the Spirit at Pentecost! According to Acts 1:14, after Jesus ascended to heaven, the apostles "continued with one accord in prayer and supplication, with the women and Mary the mother of Jesus, and with His brothers." James, Simon, Joses, and Jude, no longer antagonistic, had come to believe in Him as Messiah and Lord.

What had produced this miracle? How had His recalcitrant brothers—and James in particular—come to saving faith so that they joined the ranks of those who followed Jesus? The amazing answer is found in 1 Corinthians 15, where Paul surveyed the post-resurrection appearances of our Lord:

> For I delivered to you first of all that which I also received: that Christ died for our sins according to the Scriptures, and that He was buried, and that He rose again the third day according to the Scriptures, and that He was seen by Cephas [Peter], then by the twelve. After that He was seen by over five hundred brethren at once, of whom the greater part remain to the present, but some have fallen asleep. After that He was seen by James, then by all the apostles. (vv. 3–7)

As this passage explains, Jesus personally appeared after His resurrection to James (and possibly to the other brothers also). What a stunning reunion that must have been! Undoubtedly, it was the moment of James's conversion and explains why he was among the believers in the upper room. He had seen the resurrected Christ and confessed his brother as Lord!

So James—the stubbornly skeptical second-born son of Mary—came all the way to saving faith in his older half-brother, the Lord Jesus Christ, through a post-resurrection appearance. Thus James was there when the church was founded on the Day of Pentecost, and it would not be long before he would rise to a strategic leadership role. Jesus' other brothers, too, became instrumental members of the early church. Jude, for example, would write the New Testament epistle that bears his name.

The New Testament does not reveal much about the personal life of James. He was from Nazareth, of course. We can guess that, like Jesus, he was trained as a carpenter under the tutelage of his father Joseph. As a Galilean, he spoke not only Aramaic but also Greek—which explains the excellent Greek found in his epistle. From Paul's statement in 1 Corinthians 9:5, we also learn that he was married.

Although he had known Jesus for over three decades, he did not believe in Him until his risen brother graciously appeared to him and saved him. At the establishment of the church, James was poised for usefulness in ministry.

A PILLAR IN THE CHURCH

After the inauguration of the church on the Day of Pentecost, because the twelve apostles were frequently away preaching the gospel, James eventually became the preeminent leader of the church in Jerusalem. To borrow a contemporary term, he became its *lead pastor*.

A couple of New Testament passages allude to the vital position into which James was placed. For example, three years after Paul's conversion, and about five years after Pentecost, the former Pharisee went secretly to Jerusalem to see some of the church's foremost leaders. Significantly, he met only with Peter and "James, the Lord's brother" (Galatians 1:18–19). Several years later, when Peter was miraculously released from prison, he instructed the believers who had prayed for him to "Go, tell these things to James and to the brethren" (Acts 12:17). Because James had become the focal point of the church leadership at Jerusalem, any significant church-related matters needed to go through him.

James's leadership was made explicit at the pivotal Jerusalem

Council, which settled a major theological controversy in the early church regarding the essence of the gospel. It was stimulated when, in AD 49, after completing their first missionary journey, Paul and Barnabas came into conflict with legalistic teachers who insisted that Gentile Christians must practice certain aspects of Judaism in order to be saved. According to Acts 15:1, "Certain men came down from Judea and taught the brethren, 'Unless you are circumcised according to the custom of Moses, you cannot be saved.'" These false teachers, known in church history as the *Judaizers*, were combining the works of the Mosaic Law with the grace of the gospel. As a result, they were destroying grace (cf. Romans 11:6) and preaching another gospel altogether (Galatians 1:8–9).

The issue was obviously critical since it dealt with the very heart of the gospel and salvation. So a council was called, and Paul with Barnabas traveled to Jerusalem in order to meet with the twelve apostles and the church leaders in Jerusalem. With reference to this visit, Paul described James as one of the "pillars" of the church (Galatians 2:9), alongside the apostles Peter and John.

Acts 15:4–30 details the specific role James played in giving direction to the Jerusalem Council. After Paul and Barnabas related the salvation that God was granting to the Gentiles, as the gospel of grace was preached to them (v. 4), hostile Jewish legalists countered with these demands: "It is necessary to circumcise them, and to command them to keep the law of Moses" (v. 5). That emphasis on works again brought the crux of the argument into focus. So "the apostles and elders came together to consider this matter" (v. 6).

A lengthy debate and discussion ensued, after which the apostle Peter expressed the decision of the Council—stating that all believers, whether Jew or Gentile, are saved by grace through faith alone. In verses 7–11, Peter explained,

Men and brethren, you know that a good while ago God chose among us, that by my mouth the Gentiles should hear the word of the gospel and believe. So God, who knows the heart, acknowledged them by giving them the Holy Spirit, just as He did to us, and made no distinction between us and them, purifying their hearts by faith. Now therefore, why do you test God by putting a yoke on the neck of the disciples which neither our fathers nor we were able to bear? But we believe that through the grace of the Lord Jesus Christ we shall be saved in the same manner as they.

As Peter's statement makes clear, sinners are forgiven and reconciled to God through faith; salvation is granted by God's sovereign grace, not by man's observance of the works of the Law.

When Peter had finished speaking, James also gave a response that carried the full weight of authority, not only because he was the leader of the Jerusalem church and the one presiding over the council, but because it was the Holy Spirit who had guided the decision of the council (v. 28). James's words echoed those of Peter, rejoicing in the fact that the Lord had "visited the Gentiles to take out of them a people for His name" (v. 14). With the council's decision finalized, James sent Paul and Barnabas back to Antioch with a letter, informing the Gentile Christians of the Spirit's leading in their discussion. The clear verdict was that salvation did not require them to be circumcised nor to observe the Law of Moses (v. 24).

Even at this early stage in the life of the church, the gospel of divine grace had come under attack from those who insisted on a false system of legalistic works. The Holy Spirit used the leadership of the Jerusalem church to defend the truth about salvation. At the very center of that defense was James, the brother of Jesus.

James' prominence in the Jerusalem church is highlighted one last time in Acts 21:18. Almost a decade after the Jerusalem Council, Paul returned to Jerusalem (around AD 57). This time he was to be arrested, imprisoned, and eventually sent to Rome for trial. But when he first arrived in the city, Paul met with "James, and all the elders" of the Jerusalem church to report what God was doing among the Gentiles. Once again, we see James's leadership position in the church clearly demonstrated.

James is not mentioned again in the record of Acts. But according to church tradition, he was martyred around AD 62. When the Roman procurator Porcius Festus died, there was a brief time gap before the next Roman governor could be installed in Judea. During that transition period, the Jewish high priest took advantage of the lack of imperial oversight and had James arrested under the authority of the Sanhedrin. The notable Christian leader was then accused and convicted of breaking the law and sentenced to die. According to ancient accounts, James was thrown off the edge of the temple, then stoned and beaten to death by an angry mob.

In looking back over his life, it is difficult to overstate the strategic importance of James's influence. He led the infant church during a very tense and critical time. The church was newly born and emerging out of Judaism. Many Jewish Christians were still holding on to elements of their religious past such as going to the temple to participate in the ceremonies, festivals, and activities so familiar to them. But a shift toward freedom was slowly taking place. Moreover, believers were starting to reach Gentiles with the gospel. In so doing, they wanted to emphasize the liberty that exists in Christ, but without offending overly scrupulous Jews. It's little wonder that there was confusion surrounding the law during this period of transition from Israel to the church.

James's ministry, along with the twelve apostles, was critical in setting the church on the right foundation. A major cornerstone in that regard came at the Jerusalem Council—where Peter, James, and the other apostles and elders clearly affirmed the gospel of grace as the true gospel.

In many ways, James was the first model pastor. Unlike the twelve apostles, who eventually left Jerusalem to take the gospel throughout the world, James never left. He stayed with the church he loved, leading it faithfully for over thirty years until the day he was killed.

His commitment to the flock under his care never wavered. He was characterized by commitment to the truth but also by compassion for the consciences of his fellow Jews who were still sensitive to the traditions of Judaism. That he had a shepherd's heart is seen not only in how he cared for the church, but also in what he wrote—the epistle that bears his name.

WRITER OF SCRIPTURE

Although there are several men named James in the New Testament, only two were prominent enough to be reasonably considered as author of such an authoritative letter as the epistle of James. The first possibility, James the son of Zebedee and brother of John, was the well-known disciple and apostle of Jesus. However, since Herod Agrippa I killed him before this epistle was written (cf. Acts 12:2), he cannot be the author.

That leaves our subject, James the brother of Jesus and leader of the Jerusalem church, as the only viable candidate for authorship, and the weight of the evidence backs up that conclusion. His relation to Jesus and to the Jerusalem church put James in a unique position of spiritual authority, befitting the author of this canonical book. Additionally, a number of unique linguistic parallels exist between James's speech in Acts 15 and the content of the epistle, strongly linking the two. And evidence from Christian leaders in early church history confirms that they believed James, the brother of Jesus, to be the author.

The epistle was written to Jewish believers who had fled from Jerusalem, probably in response to the persecution instigated by Herod around AD 44. The letter does not mention the events of Acts 15 and the Jerusalem Council, which suggests that it was written before AD 49. Thus, James likely penned this letter in the mid- to late-40s, making it the first New Testament book written, with Galatians written second (in the early 50s).

Even a quick read through the epistle of James evidences its strong emphasis on application—a characteristic that reflects the shepherding heart of its author. In fact, from this letter, we can discern at least five notable character traits about James himself.

First, James was a man of true humility. This is evident because, although he was the son of Mary, the half-brother of Jesus, and the leader of the Jerusalem church, he began his letter by describing himself simply as "a bondservant [literally, *slave*] of God and of the Lord Jesus Christ" (James 1:1). He made no mention of his familial relationships or of his prominent position in Jerusalem. Rather, he emphasized that he was the slave of God and of the Lord Jesus. What an amazing testimony, especially as a younger brother! In the Old Testament, the term *slave of God* was considered a title of honor and privilege. Such notable men as Abraham, Moses, Joshua, David, and Elijah were called by that name—indicating their whole-hearted devotion and sacrificial service to the Lord. By assuming that title, James was identifying himself with those whose value and honor came not from themselves, but from the One to whom they submitted.

Second, James was a righteous man. In fact, he is known in church history as "James the Just." Appropriately, the theme of righteous living permeates his epistle. In just five chapters, he packed fifty imperatives—repeatedly commanding his readers to embrace a life of submissive obedience to God and His Word. His letter stresses the application of truth, emphasizing the spiritual fruit that should characterize the life of every true Christian. As a pastor, James had seen the devastating effects of pride, anger, selfishness, favoritism, materialism, and divisiveness within the church. He wrote to warn his readers to avoid those sin-laden traps.

Third, James was a loving pastor. He appears as a man of great compassion and sympathy, especially toward the poor and destitute. He showed no tolerance for favoritism in the church; instead he encouraged unity within the body of Christ. The church, he wrote, ought to be a fellowship of rich and poor, in which the needs of each are met and communication is characterized by heavenly wisdom. There must be true oneness, as believers submit to their elders and faithfully pray for one another. He saw the church as a group of people who ought to humbly love one another. He even referred to them as his "beloved."

Fourth, James was a man of the Word and prayer (cf. Acts 6:4). His mastery of Scripture is seen in the fact that his short letter contains four direct quotes from the Old Testament and more than forty Old Testament allusions. It also includes a number of parallels to the Sermon on the Mount, thereby echoing the teachings of Jesus. He urged his readers to listen to and obey the Word, and not to be forgetful hearers. His commitment to prayer is emphasized at both the start and end of his letter. In chapter 1, he instructs his listeners to ask God for wisdom in the midst of trials. In chapter 5, once more in the context of sickness and trials, he urges them to pray like Elijah did, being confident that "the effective, fervent prayer of a righteous man avails much" (James 5:16). Some ancient accounts report that James himself prayed so frequently that his knees became as calloused as those of a camel!

Fifth, James was a theologian. In his one letter, he provided a theology of suffering, a theology of sin and temptation, a theology of fallenness, a theology of the demonic world, a theology of the law and faith, a theology of the church, and a theology of God and Christ. He presented Christ as the Source of wisdom, the One before whom all men and women are humbled, the One who controls all history and human destiny, the coming King, and the great Physician. He further emphasized that God is one God, the Creator of the world, the source of righteousness, the object of worship, the guide in true wisdom, the sovereign ruler, the enemy of sin and worldliness, the leader of heaven's hosts, the judge of all, and the gracious receiver of those who repent.

Though it is only five chapters long, the letter abounds with both profound truth and personal application. Its tone is both personal and pastoral—as we would expect from its author. James was a man who practiced what he preached, and who lovingly led that initial generation of believers in Jerusalem to do the same.

JAMES VERSUS PAUL?

We should end the story of James at this point, but we cannot. Why? Because James's epistle has suffered needless but strong attacks from critics through the years. Though James—along with Peter and the other apostles—at the Jerusalem Council clearly affirmed the gospel of grace preached by Paul and Barnabas, some skeptics have suggested that, in reality, James and Paul were at odds in their gospel theology.

The controversy centers on the issue of faith. Paul, in Romans 3:28, explained that "a man is justified by faith apart from the deeds of the law." He reiterated that same truth in Ephesians 2 and Titus 3. But in James 2:24, James concluded "that a man is justified by works, and not by faith only." At first glance, it appears that Paul and James are teaching opposite truths. So how are believers to make sense of the apparent contradiction?

The tension is immediately alleviated when we realize that Paul was discussing the *essence* or *root* of justification (with regard to the believer's standing before God), whereas James was addressing the *evidence* or *results* of justification (with regard to the believer's life after conversion). On the one hand, sinners are saved by grace through faith in Christ alone. That was Paul's point, and James agreed with him (cf. James 1:17–18). In fact, that was the issue resolved at the Jerusalem Council in Acts 15. On the other hand, those who are truly saved will demonstrate in their lives the fruits of repentance; if their lives are fruitless, their profession of faith is false. That was James's point, and Paul would have readily concurred with that (cf. Romans 6:1, 15). Paul and James were in perfect agreement with one another; they were merely emphasizing two sides of the same reality: *faith* and its *fruit*. As Paul explained in Ephesians 2:8–10:

For by grace you have been saved through faith, and that not of yourselves; it is the gift of God, not of works, lest anyone should boast. For we are His workmanship, created in Christ Jesus for good works, which God prepared beforehand that we should walk in them.

By emphasizing both *faith* and the *fruits of repentance*, both Paul and James were echoing the teaching of Jesus. Paul's focus on *faith* reiterated the truth of Matthew 5:3: "Blessed are the poor in spirit, For theirs is the kingdom of heaven." As the Lord told Nicodemus, "For God so loved the world that He gave His only begotten Son, that whoever believes in Him should not perish but have everlasting life" (John 3:16). James's emphasis on *fruit* had the ring of Matthew 7:21: "Not everyone who says to Me, 'Lord, Lord,' shall enter the kingdom of heaven; but he who does the will of My Father who is in heaven." A few verses earlier, Jesus described human behavior with these words: "You will know them by their fruits. . . . Every good tree bears good fruit, but a bad tree bears bad fruit" (Matthew 7:16–17).

Again, there is no discrepancy between the writings of Paul and James. Paul declared that righteous deeds cannot save us. James stated that if there are no righteous deeds, we haven't been saved. In other words, both James and Paul saw good works as the *proof* of salvation—not the *means* to salvation. Their meetings in Acts 15 and 21 confirm the fact that any supposed contradiction between them exists only in the minds of the skeptics.

AN UNLIKELY HERO

In some ways, we might expect the half-brother of Jesus to be an influential leader in the early church. After all, he grew up as a part of that most privileged family.

In James's case, however, his familiarity with Jesus was for a long time the greatest obstacle to his salvation. Like his neighbors in Nazareth, James was filled with incredulity and contempt when his older half-brother claimed to be the Messiah. His skepticism was not due to any imperfection he had seen in Jesus' character, but rather to the normalness of Jesus' childhood. Perhaps James had held resentment and jealousy, probably based on the striking contrasts between him and his older sibling. Those feelings of envy became fully charged when Jesus became a popular public figure.

But the Lord had plans for James. In an act of divine grace after His resurrection, Jesus personally appeared to James. In that act of profound mercy, Christ dispelled James's doubt and derision, and he was radically transformed. When he appears in the book of Acts, he is a man with no contempt—but rather one who worships Jesus as his Lord and Savior. Ultimately, James's loving loyalty to Jesus was so strong that he gave his life as a martyr, rather than deny his brother as his Lord.

When the church was in its infancy, James was entrusted with a critical leadership role. As the transition took place, from a predominantly Jewish church to a largely Gentile church, and as the apostles ministered from place to place, a strong leader was needed to provide wisdom and stability to the elders of the church in Jerusalem. James, in the Spirit's power, did just that.

In his ministry and writings, James is sometimes pitted against the apostle Paul. In reality, however, they were both contending for the same truths. Throughout church history the greatest theological threat to the church has come in the form of attacks on the true essence of the gospel. That was the primary issue of the Protestant Reformation. It is a battle still being fought today. It was the major doctrinal debate of the early church. And James stands as a hero for providing godly leadership in the midst of that critical struggle and boldly affirming the gospel of grace, while also declaring that the Holy Spirit will produce righteous works in the lives of those people who are truly saved.

We began this chapter by asking what it must have been like to grow up with Jesus. On the flip side, we might point out that in eternity past Jesus Himself chose whom His brothers and sisters would be. As the Creator (John 1:3), He predetermined the family in which He would live for thirty years. He actually created James to be His younger half-brother, having also sovereignly chosen him to be His spiritual brother (cf. Hebrews 2:11). Jesus even designed James with the qualities he would need so that he could be given to the Jerusalem church as their first lead pastor (cf. Ephesians 4:11).

The Lord created, called, saved, and equipped James for usefulness in manifesting His glory. He does the same for all believers (Romans 8:29). Like James, we were all filled with contempt and hatred toward God at one time. But if we have come to saving faith in Christ, we too have each been forgiven and equipped for spiritual service. Our salvation has been fully secured by grace through faith in Christ. Now, as James emphasized in his epistle, we must put feet to our faith—faithfully living in submissive obedience to the Word of God. In such living, our own story will unfold to the honor of the Lord Jesus, who is not ashamed to make us part of His family (cf. Romans 8:16–17).

10
MARK AND ONESIMUS:
A TALE OF TWO RUNAWAYS

I am sending him to you . . . with Onesimus, a faithful and beloved brother, who is one of you. They will make known to you all things which are happening here. Aristarchus my fellow prisoner greets you, with Mark the cousin of Barnabas (about whom you received instructions: if he comes to you, welcome him) . . . They have proved to be a comfort to me.

—COLOSSIANS 4:8–11

ONE HUNDRED YEARS AFTER THE INFAMOUS SINKING of the *Titanic*, an Italian cruise-liner named the *Costa Concordia* struck a reef just off the coast of Italy. The collision tore a 160-foot gash in the hull of the ship. Immediately, the ship began to fill with water and soon began listing heavily to the starboard side, trapping passengers inside and making it difficult to deploy lifeboats.

Though less than three dozen lives were lost in the 2012 maritime disaster (compared to the *Titanic*'s death toll of 1,514), the story quickly gained international attention—largely due to the cowardly

189

actions of the ship's captain, Francesco Schettino. Not only was Schettino responsible for the accident, by intentionally deviating from his prescribed course and sailing much too close to the shore, he responded to the crisis by doing the unthinkable: he abandoned his ship while people were still trapped on board.

Incredibly, hundreds of passengers remained in harm's way when Schettino entered a lifeboat and sailed away from the shipwreck he had created. He tried to excuse his actions by telling authorities that he had tripped and accidentally fallen into a lifeboat; but recorded conversations between him and the Italian coast guard soon exposed a level of spinelessness that is difficult to fathom. While he waited in the safety of his lifeboat, Schettino was repeatedly told by coast guard officers to reboard his sinking ship and coordinate the rescue efforts, but the gutless captain refused. At one point, a frustrated coast guard official responded to the captain's indefensible stall tactics with utter incredulity:

> And so what? You want to go home, Schettino? It is dark and you want to go home? Get on that prow of the boat using the pilot ladder and tell me what can be done, how many people there are and what their needs are. . . . It has been an hour that you have been telling me the same thing. Now, go on board. Go on board! And then tell me immediately how many people there are there.[1]

Despite such urgings, Schettino never did return to his ship. Instead, he hid in the lifeboat, paralyzed with fear and refusing to help the very passengers he had placed in danger. Like every sea captain, he had a sworn duty to stay with his ship. Instead, filled with trepidation and shame, he abandoned his post—a coward.

Albeit negatively, Captain Schettino's shameful act underscores the essence of heroism. *Heroes*, by definition, are people who do not run away. They stay with courage and conviction to stand and face difficulty, accepting hardship and embracing self-sacrifice. They are willing, if necessary, to go down with the ship. On the other hand, those who flee in the critical moment are viewed not as heroes, but as cowards and failures.

That is what makes our final two heroes so unlikely—they were both runaways. Yet, in spite of their weaknesses and failures, the Lord rescued them; transforming their testimonies from tragedy to triumph. As He does with every sinner whom He saves, God pursued both Mark and Onesimus, and when He caught them, He turned their frailties and flaws into strength and success.

MARK: THE RESTORED DESERTER

We are introduced to Mark (or "John Mark") in the twelfth chapter of Acts. The year was around AD 45, and King Herod Agrippa I was persecuting the church in order to maintain favor with the powerful Jewish religious elites. The wicked demagogue specifically targeted the church's leadership by authorizing the public execution of James, the brother of the apostle John. When he saw that his action pleased the people, Herod also had Peter arrested and thrown into prison with the same intention.

Peter's miraculous escape from that prison is one of the most memorable accounts from the early history of the church. Chained inside a cell and watched around the clock by a squadron of Roman soldiers, he slept the night between two guards. All those elements meant to secure the apostle were useless when God wanted Peter freed. And He did. By a command of God in heaven:

> Behold, an angel of the Lord stood by him, and a light shone in the prison; and he struck Peter on the side and raised him up, saying, "Arise quickly!" And his chains fell off his hands. Then the angel said to him, "Gird yourself and tie on your sandals"; and so he did.

And he said to him, "Put on your garment and follow me." So he went out and followed him, and did not know that what was done by the angel was real, but thought he was seeing a vision. When they were past the first and the second guard posts, they came to the iron gate that leads to the city, which opened to them of its own accord; and they went out and went down one street, and immediately the angel departed from him. (Acts 12:7–10)

As Peter moved from dreaming sleep into the reality of what was happening, he found himself in a street outside the prison. Immediately, he made his way to a familiar home where some believers lived. At that very time they were praying for Peter's release. Ironically, when he knocked at the front gate, no one there believed it could actually be him. In a somewhat humorous episode, the divinely released apostle had to wait outside until those in the house finally realized that their prayers for him had been answered. According to verse 16, "Peter continued knocking; and when they opened the door and saw him, they were astonished." It had proven easier to get out of the prison than into the house of his friends.

Though it is only included as a footnote, the biblical narrative explains that this was the "house of Mary, the mother of John whose surname was Mark" (v. 12). This is the first place in Scripture that Mark's name is mentioned. (*John* was his Jewish name, while *Mark* was his Gentile name and the name most commonly associated with him.) The passage does not reveal anything more about John Mark. In fact, his name is only used to distinguish his widowed mother from the many other women named *Mary* in the New Testament.

Nonetheless, this verse reveals two important facts about Mark's life. First, it indicates that he had been raised by a devout Christian mother, whose house was a meeting place for the believers in Jerusalem. Like Timothy, who was instructed in the faith by his mother Eunice (2 Timothy 1:5), Mark had undoubtedly been reared in the truth by his mother Mary. Second, the mention of Mark's name implies a direct connection between him and Peter. After being miraculously released from prison, the apostle went to the place where he knew the church gathered—namely, Mark's mother's house. The apostle's familiarity with that house, and the family who lived there, means that Peter knew Mark. As we will see, that acquaintance would prove invaluable to the young man's later life.

MISSION FAILURE

Around the time of Peter's release, Paul and Barnabas came to Jerusalem from Antioch in Syria, the third-largest city in the Roman Empire at that time. It was there that Paul and Barnabas co-pastored a predominantly Gentile church. After taking a collection from the believers in Antioch, the ministry duo traveled south to Jerusalem, bringing much-needed provisions to the believers in Judea who were suffering through a famine (cf. Acts 11:28–30).

Once their delivery was complete, as they prepared to return to the church in Antioch, Paul (still called "Saul") and Barnabas decided to bring an extra traveler back with them. As the biblical account explains, "Barnabas and Saul returned from Jerusalem when they had fulfilled their ministry, and they took with them John whose surname was Mark" (Acts 12:25).

In Colossians 4:10, we learn that Mark was the cousin of Barnabas, which explains why he invited him to come to Antioch. Clearly, Barnabas must have trusted him, recognized his giftedness, and convinced Paul that he would be useful to their ministry among the Gentiles.

Evidently, Mark was not a preacher. Acts 13:1 lists the pastors and teachers in Antioch, and Mark's name is not included there. The fact that when Paul and Barnabas left on their first missionary journey, they took Mark with them "as their assistant" (v. 5) proves he had been useful in his brief time at Antioch. They were expecting him to further assist them as they set out to preach the gospel in Asia Minor.

From the start, the ministry faced difficulty. When they reached their first destination, the island of Paphos, a sorcerer named Elymas viciously opposed them. Paul attacked back, calling him a man of deceit, a child of the devil, and an enemy of all righteousness. In a dramatic burst of God's sovereign power, Elymas was stricken with supernatural blindness (v. 11). But as the journey continued, the missionaries experienced difficult travel and stiff resistance. Paul himself contracted a serious illness (possibly malaria) shortly after leaving Paphos (cf. Galatians 4:13–15). His infirmities undoubtedly complicated an already arduous mission.

The relentless struggles took the heart out of John Mark. Whatever the last straw, Acts 13:13 records the sad tale of his decision to abandon the mission: "Now Paul and his companions put out to sea from Paphos and came to Perga in Pamphylia; but John [Mark] left them and returned to Jerusalem" (NASB). Evidently overwhelmed by the challenges and fearful of the outcome, Mark panicked and left, not for Antioch and the church he had been serving there, but straight back to his mother's home in Jerusalem.

There was no excuse for Mark's cowardice—a fact that is confirmed in Acts 15. Several years had passed, when Paul and Barnabas decided to embark on a second missionary journey (around AD 50). As they discussed the details of their upcoming trip, Mark's abandonment came up in the planning. According to Acts 15:36–40,

> After some days Paul said to Barnabas, "Let us return and visit the brethren in every city in which we proclaimed the word of the Lord, and see how they are." Barnabas wanted to take John, called Mark, along with them also. But Paul kept insisting that they should not take him along who had deserted them in Pamphylia and had not gone with them to the work. And there occurred such a sharp disagreement that they separated from one another,

and Barnabas took Mark with him and sailed away to Cyprus. But Paul chose Silas and left, being committed by the brethren to the grace of the Lord. (NASB)

The key word in that passage is *deserted*. As Paul reminded Barnabas, Mark was a deserter, a weak-hearted soldier who flees from the field of battle.

Barnabas, with family affection for Mark, wanted to give him another opportunity. However, Paul with cold objectivity, refused to allow it. The disagreement between him and Barnabas reached opposite poles and was fixed there. It was such a severe breach over Mark that the once inseparable companions split with each other and went on separate trips.

Barnabas took Mark with him and headed to Cyprus to proclaim the gospel there. Paul replaced his former companion with Silas and traveled through Syria and Seleucia, strengthening the churches and preaching the good news. (The details of that journey are recorded in Acts 16–18.) Paul's refusal to take John Mark on a follow-up journey was certainly legitimate. The apostle's confidence had been betrayed. When it mattered most, Mark had shown that he lacked personal courage, trust in God, and fortitude. In the face of critical opportunity, he buckled and went absent without leave, abandoning his post and forsaking his mission. That kind of desertion was indefensible.

From Coward to Co-Laborer

In his classic work *The Red Badge of Courage*, nineteenth-century novelist Stephen Crane tells the compelling story of a Civil War soldier who deserted his regiment and fled from the battlefield in fear. Henry Fleming—the young Union soldier—was so ashamed at his own cowardice that he felt as though he wore "the sore badge of his dishonor." Only when he returned to his unit and fought bravely in battle did he feel like a true man.

After Mark had left Paul and Barnabas behind on that first

missionary journey, he undoubtedly suffered a similar sense of shame and disgrace that would endure until he could return to the challenge of spiritual battle again. Many months later, when Paul and Barnabas came to Jerusalem and gave glowing reports of their work (Acts 15:3–4), Mark's head must have hung low in humiliation. Undoubtedly, his heart ached deeply to return and have the opportunity to be brave and faithful—to act like a man (1 Corinthians 16:13). Paul was adamant in rejecting Mark, so even when Barnabas took him, he must have felt mixed emotions because he had fractured the powerful duo of gospel preachers. Yet like Henry Fleming, Mark would restore his reputation with the most influential and demanding apostle Paul.

After leaving with Barnabas in Acts 15:39, Mark disappeared from the annals of church history for the next decade. But that was not the end of his story. His name reemerges in a most unexpected place, roughly ten years later, when Paul, under house arrest in Rome, wrote a letter to the believers in Colossae. At the end of that epistle, he listed the names of those who were ministering to him during his imprisonment. Included in that list is none other than Mark! Paul included him along with others in a commanding tribute:

> Aristarchus my fellow prisoner greets you, with Mark the cousin of Barnabas (about whom you received instructions: if he comes to you, welcome him), and Jesus who is called Justus. These are my only fellow workers for the kingdom of God who are of the circumcision; they have proved to be a comfort to me. (Colossians 4:10–11)

Clearly something had changed in Paul's attitude toward Mark! A decade earlier, Paul had considered him an unreliable coward—a liability on a second missionary journey. Now, Mark was being extolled by the apostle as a man who ought to be gladly embraced by the Colossian believers and as a man whose companionship brought comfort and joy to him personally. In his letter to Philemon, written at the same time as Colossians, Paul included Mark as among his "fellow laborers" (Philemon 24) in the hard work of the gospel. The one-time defector was now an honored part of Paul's ministry team!

Half a dozen years later (around AD 67), Paul was imprisoned a second and final time in Rome. The faithful apostle knew martyrdom was inevitable. In his second letter to Timothy, the final inspired epistle he would ever write, Paul opened his heart to disclose that he was more than ready to die; he was eager to leave this world behind and go to receive his heavenly reward. But before he went to be with Christ, like a dying man would do, he wanted to say some personal farewells. So he asked Timothy to come visit him in prison and to bring a precious friend with him. In 2 Timothy 4:9–11, Paul told Timothy who that friend was:

> Be diligent to come to me quickly; for Demas has forsaken me, having loved this present world, and has departed for Thessalonica—Crescens for Galatia, Titus for Dalmatia. Only Luke is with me. Get Mark and bring him with you, for he is useful to me for ministry.

Once again, Paul had been deserted by one of his companions. This time by Demas, who abandoned him for the sake of worldly comforts and pursuits. Crescens and Titus were not deserters, but they left Paul to fulfill ministry responsibilities elsewhere. Only Luke was with him there in Rome.

So Paul asked Timothy to visit him and, on the way, to pick up Mark. At the time of his first imprisonment, Paul had been blessed to have Mark by his side, and at the end of his life—which had been filled with countless friends and beloved partners in ministry—he wanted to see Mark again. The apostle who had once refused him as a traveling companion chose him now to be near him in his final days.

What was it that changed Mark from a spiritual coward and

deserter into one of Paul's most loved and honored co-workers? The answer seems to be found in Mark's friendship with the other prominent apostolic preacher—Peter. We've already noted that Peter knew Mark. And if anyone understood the shame of cowardice and the process of restoration, it was Peter. He himself had been restored after denying Christ three times (cf. John 18:15–17; 21:14–17).

It turns out that it was Peter who took Mark under his wing and discipled him in the faith. How do we know that? It comes from Peter himself, at the end of his first epistle, where he writes to the church in Rome (using the cryptic term *Babylon*): "She who is in Babylon, elect together with you, greets you; and so does Mark my son" (1 Peter 5:13). Mark was not Peter's physical son. But he was his son in the faith. No doubt Mark had come to Christ while listening in his mother's house to Peter's preaching. And after Mark's meltdown in Acts 13, it was Peter whom God used to restore him to usefulness.

There's more. The testimony of church history confirms that Peter came to Rome in the early 60s and ministered there for at least a year. It is likely that he arrived after Paul's first imprisonment and that he was executed by Nero around AD 65—a year or two before Paul's second imprisonment and execution. (Paul was likely on a fourth missionary journey, traveling outside of Rome, during those intervening years.) While Peter was there, in the capital city of the empire, faithfully preaching the gospel and shepherding the Roman believers, he also wrote his two epistles to the churches of Asia Minor. So from his reference to Mark in 1 Peter 5:13, we know that they were together during that time.

What an astonishing and immense privilege Mark enjoyed—to be the companion of both Paul and Peter! As a young man, he had faltered in the field and fled in shame. But later in life he had been graciously restored to ministry usefulness—and even elevated to the sides of the two greatest apostolic preachers.

As preeminently fulfilling as that reality was, God would grant

Mark a far greater honor. He would be inspired by the Holy Spirit to write one of the four histories of the life of the Lord Jesus Christ—the gospel of Mark!

GOSPEL WRITER

Though the second gospel does not include the name of its writer, the unanimous and unequivocal testimony of church history credits its authorship to Mark. The very early church father Papias (ca. 70–155) explained that the content for Mark's gospel came from the preaching of Peter, which is consistent with what we know of their friendship. Papias wrote,

> Mark, being the recorder of Peter, wrote accurately but not in order whatever he [Peter] remembered of the things either said or done by the Lord . . . so that Mark did not err at all when he wrote certain things just as he had recalled [them]. For he had but one intention, not to leave out anything he had heard, nor to falsify anything in them. (Cited from Eusebius, *Church History*, 3.39.15–16)

Justin Martyr (ca. 100–165) similarly referred to Mark's gospel as the "memoirs of Peter." Later church fathers, such as Irenaeus, Origen, and Clement of Alexandria echo that same conclusion. The fourth-century church historian Eusebius of Caesarea (ca. 263–339) explains why Mark wrote his gospel:

> A great light of religion shone on the minds of the hearers of Peter, so that they were not satisfied with a single hearing or with the unwritten teaching of the divine proclamation, but with every kind of exhortation [they] entreated Mark, whose gospel is still in existence, seeing that he was Peter's follower, to leave them a written statement of the teaching given them verbally, nor did they cease until they had persuaded him, and so became the cause of the scripture called the Gospel according to Mark. And they

say that the Apostle, knowing by the revelation of the spirit to him what had been done, was pleased at their zeal, and ratified the scripture for study in the churches. (*Church History*, 2.15.1–2)

As Eusebius explained, based on the information available to him, it was the early Christians who prevailed upon Mark to write down the teachings of Peter. Mark, then, was inspired by the Holy Spirit to accomplish that sacred task, and the result has been preserved for us in the New Testament.

The theme of Mark's gospel is found in the middle of the six-teen-chapter history. Mark 8:29 records Peter's answer to Jesus' question, "Who do you say that I am?" Peter rightly responded, "You are the Christ." That confession is the pinnacle of the book. Everything before it leads up to it, and everything after flows from it. The first eight chapters prove that Jesus is the Christ on account of His deeds and words, the second eight on account of His death and resurrection. But everything orbits around that central theological reality: *The Lord Jesus is the Christ, the Messiah, and the only Savior.*

Thus the gospel of Mark is an evangelistic book. It has the same objective as John's gospel—that those who read it would believe in Jesus Christ and have life in His name (John 20:31). Mark's gospel was written to draw sinners out of their confusion and hostility to the saving Person of Jesus Christ. How appropriately ironic that the man who had once abandoned his evangelistic responsibilities by deserting Paul and Barnabas on their first missionary journey would one day write a gospel that has since reached billions of people with the good news of salvation.

The man who may have never preached a sermon proclaims Jesus as Lord and Christ every moment to human history so that he is always a human instrument in the salvation of sinners. He was an ordinary man, characterized by sin, weakness, and failure. Yet God gave him privilege beyond calculation—not only as a friend of Paul and a student of Peter—but infinitely more as the human author of the divinely inspired gospel that forever bears his name.

ONESIMUS: THE FORGIVEN FUGITIVE

While Mark was with Paul in Rome, during the apostle's first imprisonment, he was in the company of a young man named Onesimus. Though they came from very different backgrounds, the two shared a common feature: in the past, they had both deserted their responsibility and run away. Mark had been a runaway missionary; Onesimus, a runaway slave. Yet in God's perfect providence, both men found themselves together in Rome, in the companionship of the most powerful instrument of God, the apostle Paul.

Onesimus was not a believer when he violated Roman law and disdained the care of his master—Philemon, a Christian man who lived in Colossae. It is safe to assume, because Philemon was a believer and a leader in the Colossian church, that he was a gracious and fair master (cf. Philemon 5). But Onesimus wanted his freedom and found an opportunity to snatch it.

Fleeing to Rome like other fugitives, he hoped to be lost among the masses that thronged the imperial capital. (Historical estimates place the population of Rome at that time around eight hundred seventy thousand people.) But he could not hide from the One who was seeking his soul. Though the circumstances are not revealed, God brought Onesimus to Paul—and to the gospel of freedom found in the Lord Jesus.

Surely, Onesimus had heard Paul's name when he was still at his master's home in Colossae. The church met there. Philemon may have even taken him to hear Paul preach when the apostle was in nearby Ephesus. Perhaps, after Onesimus came to Rome, the Spirit of God convicted him of his sin, and he sought out the apostle for help. Whatever the explanation for their meeting, one thing is clear:

once Onesimus met Paul, his life was permanently changed because through Paul he met the Lord Jesus.

Onesimus, whose name means "useful," quickly became one of Paul's beloved and eager students (Philemon 12, 16). He willingly served the imprisoned apostle (vv. 11, 13) so effectively that Paul wished he could keep Onesimus with him. But there was a critical matter that needed to be settled—legally, relationally, and spiritually.

A runaway slave was a felon—guilty of a serious crime. Onesimus was a fugitive—a wanted man in the eyes of the Roman justice system. He had not only defrauded his master of his services, but likely stolen goods or money from Philemon when he left (v. 18). Now that he had become a believer in Christ and been reconciled to God, Onesimus had no choice but to go back to his master and be restored as his slave.

The necessity of sending Onesimus back to Colossae became more urgent when Paul finished his epistle to the church in that city. Along with it, a second letter—a personal appeal from Paul to Philemon regarding the returning slave—was sent. According to Colossians 4:7–9, the apostle dispatched a man named Tychicus to deliver those letters, along with "Onesimus, a faithful and beloved brother, who is [now] one of you." Together, Tychicus and the fugitive slave headed for Colossae on their vital mission.

In his letter to Philemon, Paul explained that it was a great personal sacrifice for him to send Onesimus back to Colossae. But the potential ramifications were actually much greater for Onesimus. Under Roman law, a master could punish a runaway slave in almost any way he wanted—including putting him to death. In some cases, captured runaways were branded with an "F" (for "Fugitive") on their foreheads or severely beaten for their actions. Because slaves were expensive and valuable, and because the Romans were always wary of the possibility of a slave uprising, they often dealt harshly with rebels and runaways.

But Onesimus was willing to face his defrauded master and take that risk. Not only had he been radically transformed by Christ, he also knew the genuineness of his master's faith. Philemon would surely heed Paul's reminder in Colossians 4:1, "Masters, [remember] that you also have a Master in heaven." Onesimus undoubtedly rested in the fact that both he and Philemon ultimately served the same Master. No matter what the outcome, the right thing to do was to seek Philemon's forgiveness.

SLAVERY IN THE ROMAN EMPIRE

In order to fully comprehend the situation regarding Onesimus and Philemon, it is important to understand a little more about the institution of Roman slavery. (Those interested in learning more about this topic can find a detailed discussion of it in my book *Slave: The Hidden Truth About Your Identity in Christ*.)

Slavery was a pervasive social structure in the first-century Roman Empire. In fact, it was so commonplace that its existence as an institution was never seriously questioned by anyone. (The New Testament itself never condemns the slave-system of Roman times, teaching instead that masters must treat their slaves with kindness. Nonetheless, biblical principles eventually led to the dissolution of slavery after the Roman Empire was Christianized.)

Slaves of all ages, genders, and ethnicities constituted an important socioeconomic class in ancient Rome. Roughly one-fifth of the empire's population were slaves—totaling as many as twelve million at the outset of the first century. Not surprisingly, the entire Roman economy was highly dependent on this sizable pool of both skilled and unskilled labor.

Initially, the Roman slave population came through military conquests. As the empire expanded its borders, it captured vast numbers of people who were subsequently sold into bondage. But by the first century, the majority of slaves inherited their place in society by being born into slavery. Most slaves, then, had never known freedom, and that was likely true of Onesimus. He may have even grown up in the household of Philemon, making his departure and robbery even more unthinkable.

Because they were assured of food, clothing, and shelter, slaves were often better off than poor freemen who might go hungry or sleep in the streets. When the money he stole ran out and the reality of his destitution set in, Onesimus would have found himself hungry and homeless in the streets of Rome—discovering that the dream of freedom had turned into a nightmare. That may explain his initial desire to seek out the apostle Paul.

For many slaves, life was difficult—especially for those who worked in mines or on farms. These "rustic" slaves often lived far away from their city-dwelling owners, under the supervision of a foreman or manager. But there were also many slaves who lived in the cities, working alongside their masters as part of the household. For these "urban" slaves, like Onesimus, life was often considerably easier (especially for someone who served in a Christian household).

Depending on their training and on their masters' needs, slaves functioned in numerous capacities—both inside and outside the home. From teachers to cooks to shopkeepers to doctors, slaves were involved in a wide variety of occupations. From a glance on the street, it would have been difficult to distinguish between slaves and non-slaves. There was essentially no difference in dress; neither were there significant differences in functions. Any line of work a free person might do, a slave might also do. Onesimus's usefulness to Paul may have been an extension of his training as a slave. Perhaps Onesimus prepared meals for Paul or provided him with medical attention (alongside Luke) or served as a personal assistant in some way.

Household slaves received greater honor than other slaves because they worked more closely with their masters. As members of the household, they were intimately involved in every part of family life—from taking care of the master's children to managing his house or even administrating his business interests. A wicked slave was a great liability and could cause serious damage to the owner's welfare. But a loyal and hardworking slave was an unparalleled asset. When Onesimus fled, he had shown himself to be a wicked slave. His return, however, was as a sinner transformed by grace.

The faithful slave could actually expect to receive his freedom one day—a reward that owners often used to motivate their slaves toward full compliance. By New Testament times, manumission (the releasing of slaves) had become so common that the Roman government had to regulate it. Oftentimes, masters would release their slaves upon their death, stating manumission as part of their last will and testament. But even though freedom for slaves was becoming more common, slaves who ran away as Onesimus did faced the threat of dire consequences.

PAUL'S LETTER TO PHILEMON

Though it was several years earlier, Philemon—like his slave—had been saved through the preaching of Paul, probably during the apostle's ministry in nearby Ephesus. Philemon was a true believer, whom Paul refers to as a "beloved friend and fellow laborer" (Philemon 1). He was wealthy enough to own a large house where the Colossian church met (v. 2), and where he ministered as a prominent member. His wife Apphia and son Archippus had also been converted; and surely all three had urged Onesimus to embrace the gospel.

Furthermore, as an "urban" slave, Onesimus would have been his master's close companion, a familiar member of the household staff. Philemon no doubt implicitly trusted and generously cared for him. But his kindness had been repaid with treachery. Lest Philemon respond harshly toward Onesimus whom God had forgiven, Paul sent a letter urging him to forgive his runaway slave and receive him as a brother in Christ.

Though the letter to Philemon is short, its theme is one of the most far-reaching in all of Scripture: *forgiveness*. In his epistle to the church at Colossae, the apostle wrote, "Put on tender mercies, kindness, humility, meekness, longsuffering; bearing with one another, and forgiving one another, if anyone has a complaint against another; even as Christ forgave you, so you also must do" (Colossians 3:12–13). His letter to Philemon applied that principle of Christ-like forgiveness to this specific situation.

The book of Philemon begins by focusing on the spiritual character of forgiving people. They are marked by a love both for the Lord and for others (v. 5). They not only profess their faith in Christ, but they also demonstrate the reality of that faith in how they live (v. 6). And the generous nature of their love refreshes all those who know them (v. 7). Paul was confident that Philemon was characterized by these spiritual traits.

In the next section of the letter (vv. 8–18), the apostle explained how Philemon ought to respond to Onesimus. In a particularly personal and poignant way, Paul appealed on behalf of the runaway slave, with these words:

> Therefore, though I might be very bold in Christ to command you what is fitting, yet for love's sake I rather appeal to you— being such a one as Paul, the aged, and now also a prisoner of Jesus Christ—I appeal to you for my son Onesimus, whom I have begotten while in my chains, who once was unprofitable to you, but now is profitable to you and to me. I am sending him back. You therefore receive him, that is, my own heart, whom I wished to keep with me, that on your behalf he might minister to me in my chains for the gospel. But without your consent I wanted to do nothing, that your good deed might not be by compulsion, as it were, but voluntary. For perhaps he departed for a while for this purpose, that you might receive him forever, no longer as a slave but more than a slave—a beloved brother,

especially to me but how much more to you, both in the flesh and in the Lord. If then you count me as a partner, receive him as you would me. But if he has wronged you or owes anything, put that on my account.

Notably, Paul's request to Philemon was founded on the fact that both he and Onesimus were brothers in Christ. On that basis, Philemon ought to receive his runaway slave as he would receive any other believer, including Paul himself. The goal was not merely to forego punishment, but to offer genuine reconciliation and the restoration of a violated relationship.

Finally, Paul ended his appeal by reminding Philemon of his spiritual heritage—that, like Onesimus, he too had been saved from slavery to sin under Paul's evangelistic ministry (vv. 19–25). The apostle was confident that Philemon would obey and in so doing would bring the apostle the joy of encouragement. And Philemon's righteous response would serve as a mighty testimony to grace received and given.

FROM RUNAWAY SLAVE TO CHURCH LEADER

The implication of Paul's letter, supported by the testimony of church history, is that Philemon responded exactly as Paul expected he would. According to ancient tradition, after they reconciled, Philemon sent Onesimus back to Paul, where he continued to serve and minister to the apostle.

Though the story is certainly touching, one might wonder why this brief letter is included in the New Testament. After all, it is the shortest of Paul's epistles. It was written to an individual, not to a church. It does not address any complex theological issues. And it deals with an aspect of Roman culture, namely slavery, that died out in church history.

In response, two primary reasons can be given for its inclusion. First, a spiritual reason—the theme of forgiveness is one that the Holy Spirit knew every Christian needs to grasp. According to Ephesians 5:1, believers become the "imitators of God" when they forgive other people. The reality is that we are never more like our Savior than when we show grace and mercy to those who do not deserve it. God has forgiven us based on the finished work of Christ. When we forgive others, we reflect His loving character and demonstrate that we are indeed His children.

But there is also a historical reason, from the human perspective, for the inclusion of this book in the biblical canon. Around AD 110, an early Christian leader named Ignatius, the bishop of Antioch, wrote a letter to the church at Ephesus. In that letter, he addressed the bishop of Ephesus multiple times—repeatedly noting that the leader of the Ephesian church was a man named Onesimus!

Could this be the same Onesimus as Philemon's runaway and reconciled slave? There are good reasons to think so. Paul's epistle to Philemon was written five decades before Ignatius's letter to the Ephesians. If Onesimus were a young man (in his early twenties) when Paul wrote (around AD 61), he would have been in his early seventies when Ignatius penned his letter. That age would certainly be appropriate for a bishop in the early church. But there is an even more compelling reason to make this connection, as renowned New Testament scholar F. F. Bruce explains:

> Why, then, should one connect the Onesimus who was bishop of Ephesus about AD 110 with the Onesimus who figures in the letter of Philemon between fifty and sixty years earlier?
>
> Because . . . Ignatius in his letter to the church of Ephesus shows himself familiar with the Epistle to Philemon; it is one of the rare places in patristic literature where the language of our epistle is clearly echoed. Not only so, but the part of Ignatius's letter to Ephesus where the language of Philemon is echoed is the part in which Bishop Onesimus is mentioned—the first six chapters. In these six chapters the bishop is mentioned fourteen times; in the

remaining fifteen chapters he is not mentioned at all, apart from one general reference: "obey the bishop and the presbytery with an undisturbed mind." This consideration is impressive, if not conclusive.[2]

The fact that Ignatius repeatedly referenced the book of Philemon in a letter to a pastor named Onesimus is strong evidence that this was the same Onesimus described in the New Testament.

Going one step further, some New Testament scholars, like Bruce, have suggested that Onesimus was likely instrumental in collecting and preserving the letters of Paul. If so, he would have made sure to include this epistle, which was written on his behalf by the honored apostle.

Obviously, God Himself sovereignly orchestrated the preservation of the canonical books which make up the New Testament. Just as the Holy Spirit inspired the apostles to pen sacred Scripture, He also ensured that their authoritative writings would be preserved for the church (cf. Isaiah 40:8; 1 Peter 1:25). Thus, God is the One who determined the canon, as He providentially worked in the hearts of believers to recognize and submit to His inspired revelation (cf. John 10:27; 1 Thessalonians 2:13).

Yet in accomplishing His providential purposes with regard to the canon, God used human instruments. It seems likely that Onesimus was one of them—as he helped to gather the letters of Paul into one place. If so, that certainly qualifies him as an unlikely hero. A former runaway slave, he was restored and forgiven, eventually becoming a significant Christian pastor and a force in the early development of the New Testament canon. That is an amazing story, and a true testimony to God's grace!

Church tradition suggests that Onesimus was a servant to Paul and the other apostles until their deaths. Then he preached the gospel in places like Spain and Colossae before becoming the pastor in Ephesus. He was reportedly martyred during the reign of Emperor

Trajan for his refusal to deny Christ. This former slave of men had become a slave of Christ. As the witness of church history indicates, Onesimus faithfully served his heavenly Master to the very end.

COMPARING THESE TWO RUNAWAYS

When we compare the lives of Mark and Onesimus, we see a number of striking similarities.

- Mark was the son of a Christian woman in Jerusalem. Onesimus was the slave of a Christian family in Colossae.
- Mark ran away from the mission field in order to go back home. Onesimus ran away from home to go to a place where he became part of the mission field.
- Mark was restored to ministry and comforted Paul during the apostle's first Roman imprisonment. Onesimus was converted by Paul during that same imprisonment, and he also ministered to the apostle.
- Mark is mentioned by Paul in Colossians 4:10. Onesimus is mentioned in Colossians 4:9, just one verse earlier. Obviously Mark and Onesimus were together with Paul in Rome.
- According to church tradition, after Peter and Paul died, Mark went on to become the pastor of the church in Alexandria. Onesimus went on to become the pastor of the church in Ephesus. Eventually, both were martyred for their unwavering faith in Jesus Christ.
- Under the inspiration of the Holy Spirit, Mark collected and preserved the preaching of Peter by writing Peter's memoirs in his gospel account. Under the providential direction of the Spirit, Onesimus helped to collect and preserve the teachings of Paul by gathering Paul's letters into one place to help form the New Testament.

The impact of these men is incalculable. Only the Lord knows the full extent of their usefulness to the souls of multiplied millions through all history.

Although Mark and Onesimus were both *runaways*, they were transformed by God into *heroes* of early church history. It may be true that heroes, by definition, are people who do not run away. But as we have seen in the lives of these two men, God is in the business of changing defectors from weak vessels into powerful agents of His revelation and salvation. For Mark, the restored deserter, and Onesimus, the forgiven fugitive, the story of their lives points clearly to the One who rescued them, refusing to let them go even when they tried to run away. What joy there is for us as believers—to know that in spite of all our failings, we can never outrun God's grace or His plan to use us far beyond what we could ask or imagine.

Epilogue

OUR STUDY OF THE HEROES OF THE FAITH has shown us that the Lord does not limit His kingdom work to one kind of person. In fact, no two are the same, demonstrating that God uses almost endless combinations of personality, cultural background, experience, and station in society to accomplish His will. He is not limited by age (Enoch lived for 365 years; John the Baptist for about 30); status (Jonathan was a prince; Onesimus was a slave); human strength (Gideon was a weak coward; Samson was supernaturally strong); or even past sins (Paul persecuted the church; John Mark was a deserter; and Jonah rebelled against God's command).

Moreover, our survey has taken us on a journey through the chronology of biblical history. In every epoch, the Lord used faithful people to accomplish great things for His glory. Enoch lived before the Flood. Joseph was born after that great judgment in the patriarchal age. Miriam experienced the exodus of God's nation from Egypt. Gideon and Samson were both judges in Israel. Jonathan was the son of Saul, Israel's first king. Jonah was a prophet who ministered during the divided monarchy of Israel and Judah. Esther ruled as a queen in Persia after the Babylonian captivity. John the Baptist broke four hundred years of silence by announcing the coming of the Messiah. James, the brother of Jesus, helped lead the early church. Finally, Mark and Onesimus served as second generation leaders of the church after the apostles. From the earliest points of human history (before the Flood) to the earliest points of church history (the generation after the apostles), God has been at work in the lives of His people through unlikely heroes.

As different as these twelve were, they shared two common qualities. First, they demonstrated *faith in the Lord*. Whether facing dangerous circumstances or deadly consequences, they put their hope in God, resting in Him for salvation and embracing the promises of His Word. Rather than walking by sight, and clinging tightly to the temporal things of this world, they set their gaze on heaven and the future reward that God has promised to all who are His (Hebrews 11:16). They did not rest in their own wisdom or strength, but relied fully on God—who utilized them to achieve His purposes.

Second, they responded in *faithfulness to the Lord*, putting feet to their faith and living obediently. Enoch's faith is seen in the fact that he walked with God for three hundred years in the midst of a wicked society. Joseph trusted in God's sovereign wisdom and providence so firmly that he willingly forgave the brothers who had betrayed him. In Miriam's case, she saw her faith rewarded when the exodus from Egypt finally came, and she responded in leading praise on the shores of the Red Sea. Though she had sinned against her brother Moses in the wilderness, Miriam ended her life quietly submitting to God's plan by supporting his leadership.

Gideon put his trust in God's power, suppressing his fears and leading his tiny army to fight the Midianites. For most of his life, Samson sinfully relied on his own strength, which got him into serious trouble. Finally, at the very end, he cried out in dependence on the Lord; and God granted him a major victory over the Philistines.

Jonathan's faith was tested when he learned he would never be the king; yet, the prince gladly embraced God's plans for him and for his best friend, the chosen king—David. The prophet Jonah tried to run away from God but repented while in the belly of a fish, was delivered, and preached to Nineveh so that the entire city was saved. Queen Esther initiated a three-day fast, which included prayers of trust in the Lord; afterward, she put her faith into action by risking her life and pleading for her people.

John the Baptist renounced the worldly trappings of his day and passionately called Israel to repentance from the Judean wilderness. After coming to saving faith, James became a significant leader in the Jerusalem church; his epistle emphasizes the theme of faith in action. Mark showed cowardice and weakness, yet later demonstrated strong faithfulness in assisting both Peter and Paul. And Onesimus, the runaway slave, became useful to Paul and eventually served as the pastor of the church in Ephesus.

None of these heroes were perfect, of course. Their sins and failings are recorded—some with more detail than others—and all for our admonition (1 Corinthians 10:8–11). The sins of the saints in Scripture are always recounted with simple candor and never in a way that excuses or glorifies the wrongdoing. While standing as a rebuke to our sin, such stories also comfort us with the reminder that throughout history, God has used imperfect vessels, "that the excellence of the power may be of God and not of us" (2 Corinthians 4:7). After all, Christ came to seek and to save the lost—not the righteous, but sinners (Luke 19:10; Mark 2:17). These unlikely heroes all depict the truth of that promise, and that reality serves as a rich encouragement to all believers. If God didn't use imperfect people, He wouldn't have anyone to use.

All that notwithstanding, the truth is that left to themselves, in their sins and failings, none of these individuals would have been heroes in God's kingdom. Yet, in His wisdom and power, God accomplished heroic feats through them. He is the true Hero in every story. He brought Enoch home to heaven without dying. He orchestrated the events of Joseph's life behind the scenes for the preservation of Israel. With massive miracles, He delivered Miriam and her fellow Hebrews from Egypt. He gave Israel's enemies into the hands of Gideon and Samson. He honored Jonathan's commitment to David. He preserved Jonah in the belly of the fish. He directed the heart of Ahasuerus to desire Esther and hear her pleas. He appointed John the Baptist to be Christ's forerunner, and created James to be His brother. And He restored both Mark and Onesimus to places of usefulness—employing Mark to record the teachings of Peter and Onesimus to collect the writings of Paul. In every story, God was undeniably at work; His hand of providence was everywhere present. The same is true for us today. We can trust Him, knowing that "all things work together for good to those who love God, to those who are the called according to His purpose" (Romans 8:28).

Though we may never experience the same extraordinary exploits as these heroes of the faith, the principles and powerful providences that characterized their lives are still going on among us as well. We are called to lead lives of steadfast faith in the Lord. We are further commanded to live in faithful obedience to Him. To borrow a phrase from a well-known lyric, we must "trust and obey." When we do, we can be confident that God will use us to accomplish His purposes for His glory. As believers, there can be no greater joy than knowing that we are "sanctified and useful for the Master, prepared for every good work" (2 Timothy 2:21).

A life of faith-filled obedience probably won't win you any accolades in this world characterized by enmity toward God. Faithful Christian living often results in persecution, not praise. But rest assured, God's promises are true. One day your faith will become sight (1 Corinthians 13:12) and your faithfulness will be rewarded (Matthew 25:21, 23). In this world, those who live by faith and walk in faithfulness are often derided and despised. But in the world to come, they will be greeted with nothing less than a hero's welcome.

ACKNOWLEDGMENTS

———

A S WITH THE PREVIOUS TWO BOOKS IN THIS SERIES, *Twelve Ordinary Men* and *Twelve Extraordinary Women*, I could not have done this alone. Special thanks to Nathan Busenitz, who compiled and edited the contents of the first draft from my sermons, commentaries, and study notes—supplementing the material with additional research and writing where necessary, then presenting it to me for further work to reach a final product. Thanks, on the other end, to Brian Hampton, Bryan Norman, and the whole team at Thomas Nelson for their help, encouragement, and patience while this book was in the works. Thanks also to my son, Matt, whose assistance in publishing has been a great blessing to me personally.

217

NOTES

~~~

Chapter 10

1. The Associated Press. "Transcript: Costa Concordia Captain and Italian Coast Guard." *USA Today* (01/17/2012). Accessed, March 30, 2012, http://travel.usatoday.com/cruises/story/2012-01-17/Transcript -Costa-Concordia-captain-and-Italian-coast-guard/52613814/1.
2. F. F. Bruce, *Paul: Apostle of the Heart Set Free* (Grand Rapids: Eerdmans, 2000), 402.

About the Author

W IDELY KNOWN for his thorough, candid approach to teaching God's Word, John MacArthur is a popular author and conference speaker and has served as pastor-teacher of Grace Community Church in Sun Valley, California, since 1969. John and his wife, Patricia, have four grown children and fifteen grandchildren.

John's pulpit ministry has been extended around the globe through his media ministry, Grace to You, and its satellite offices in seven countries. In addition to producing daily radio programs for nearly two thousand English and Spanish radio outlets worldwide, Grace to You distributes books, software, audiotapes, and CDs by John MacArthur.

John is president of the Master's College and Seminary and has written hundreds of books and study guides, each one biblical and practical. Best-selling titles include *The Gospel According to Jesus*, *The Truth War*, *The Murder of Jesus*, *Twelve Ordinary Men*, *Twelve Extraordinary Women*, and *The MacArthur Study Bible*, a 1998 ECPA Gold Medallion recipient.

For more details about John MacArthur and his Bible-teaching resources, contact Grace to You at 800-55-GRACE or www.gty.org.

9781400204151-C